STANDING TALL

THE STORY OF GOSPEL MUSIC'S
WILLIAMS BROTHERS

BY THE WILLIAMS BROTHERS
WITH GLEN ALLISON

BILLBOARD BOOKS

*An imprint of Watson-Guptill Publications
New York*

Senior Editor: Bob Nirkind
Production Manager: Hector Cambell
Book and cover design: Derek Bacchus

Copyright © 1999 by The Williams Brothers

First published in the United States in 1999 by Watson-Guptill
Publications, 1515 Broadway, New York, N.Y. 10036

Library of Congress Cataloging-in-Publication Data
Still standing tall: the story of gospel music's Williams Brothers /
    the Williams Brothers with Glen Allison.
        p.   cm.
    Discography.   p.
    ISBN 0-8230-7685-7
    1. Williams Brothers (Gospel group)   2. Gospel musicians—
United States—Biography. I. Allison, Glen. II. Williams Brothers
(Gospel group)
ML 421.W53A3   1999
782.25′4′0922–dc21
[B]   98-54071
                                                              CIP
                                                              MN

All rights reserved. No part of this publication may be reproduced or
used in any form or by any means—graphic, electronic, or mechanical,
including photocopying, recording, taping, or information storage and
retrieval systems—without written permission of the publisher.

Manufactured in the United States of America

First printing, 1999

1 2 3 4 5 6 7 8 9 / 07 06 05 04 03 02 01 00 99

BOBBY JONES

> *Host and producer,* Bobby Jones
> Gospel / Video Gospel,
> *Black Entertainment Television*

The Williams Brothers have made a tremendous contribution to not only the Gospel music industry but to the world music industry as well. . . . They are leaders in this great army for the Lord. What more could you ask for? The legacy of the Williams Brothers will live throughout our lifetime and for future generations to come.

THE REV. JESSE L. JACKSON, SR.

The Williams Brothers have been able to turn pain into power. As Dr. King said, "They have carved out of the mountain of despair a stone of hope." In the desert they have found a water hole. Let all of us read, listen, and rejoice.

K-CI AND JOJO HAILEY

I would like to give the highest respect to The Williams Brothers in their contribution to Gospel music and also as role models to every young Gospel Quartet Group. . . . They inspired me and my brother in many ways, letting us know what brotherly love really is and with God's help it is "Lasting Love."

STEVLAND MORRIS (STEVIE WONDER)

Back in the day it would have been said, "Boy you can't have no secular artist singing on your gospel record" as if people who sang songs about relationships between man and woman, love, and conditions in the world were not pure enough to give praise to God for Him giving us life, love, joy, peace, and positive vision. But thanks to people like The Williams Brothers and other gospel groups and artists, we have all grown to understand that praising God must reach in every place that there are the living. We must celebrate in song His Holy Name.

Thanks for bringing us together as a family.

EVANDER HOLYFIELD

The Williams Brothers are one of my favorite gospel groups. One song in particular comes to mind as being my mother's favorite as well as mine. I have fond memories of listening to my mother sing: *I'm just a nobody / Trying to tell everybody / About somebody who can save anybody.*

I would like to say thanks for the memories to The Williams Brothers and keep up the good work with your music ministry.

STILL STANDING TALL

THE STORY OF GOSPEL MUSIC'S
WILLIAMS BROTHERS

THIS BOOK IS DEDICATED TO

Mrs. Amanda "Mom" Williams
Mrs. Ruth Green
Mrs. Inez Jackson

And to the memory of

Leon "Pop" Williams
Frank Williams
Harvey Watkins, Sr.
Rev. James Cleveland
Ed Smith
Willie Banks
Johnny Martin
Rev. Herman Brown
Rev. Milton Brunson
Theo "Bless My Bones" Wade
"Hoss Man" Allen

ACKNOWLEDGMENTS

Over the course of our 36 plus years in the gospel music ministry, traveling all across this country and abroad, so many unique and extraordinary people have crossed our paths and touched our lives in so many different ways—spiritually, financially, artistically, through prayer, through encouragement, through friendship—that it would take a separate book to acknowledge them all. So the list that follows is a partial one only, a way to say thank-you to some of the people who have been important to us.

Yolanda Adams
Ralph Adcock
Gary Alford
Rosetta Anderson
Stephanie Andrews

Bill Barron
Larry Blackwell
Steve Blue
The Bolton Brothers
Amy Bolton-Curley
Eric Brice
Diane Brown
James Bullard

Shirley Caesar
Doris Cain
Bishop Fred Caldwell, Sr.
The Canton Spirituals
Bro. James Chambers
Paul Christensen
Lisa Collins
Patrick Cowart
Andraé Crouch
Paul & Jan Crouch

John Daniels
Gene Delcomyn
Hazel Denard
The Dixie Hummingbirds

Pharis Evans, Jr.
Randy Everett

Gil Few
Louis Foster
Mike Frascogna

Terrell Gatlin
Dwight Gordon
Gospel Music Workshop
    of America
Charlotte Graham
Sandra Graham
Al Green

K-Ci & JoJo Hailey
Teresa Harris
Bishop Walter Hawkins
Gene Henson
Al Hobbs

Evander Holyfield
Derrick Horne
Eddie Howard, Jr.

Jackson Southernaires
Don Jackson
Rev. Jesse Jackson
Bishop T.D. Jakes
Willie Neal Johnson/
    Gospel Keynotes
Dr. Bobby Jones
Rev. Ed Jones
Bishop Noel Jones

John P. Kee
Pastor Ronald Kimble

Pastor James Lee
Joe Ligon/Mighty Clouds
    of Joy
Bishop Tommie Lockett
Ralph Lofton

Bob MacKenzie
Malaco Records

Jerry Mannery
Jerry Masters
Brenadé Maxwell
George McClain
Sis. Mattie McCulloch
Jane McElveen
Mississippi Mass Choir
Bill Morris
Bishop Paul S. Morton, Sr.

Sensational Nightingales

Gary Oliver

Duranice Pace
Bishop Murphy Pace III
Sis. Ricci Phillips
Bill Pinkney
Pastor Brandon Porter
Paul Porter

Ouida Rainey
Amanda Ramsey
John Ray
Carla Reed
John Rogers
Kenton Rogers
Rev. John E. Rucker
Wilton Rushing

Thomas Saulsberry
Jerry Smith/Children
    of Israel
Joel Smith
Tim Smith
Joe Sones
Candi Staton
Bro. Robert Stevenson
Rev. George Stewart

Telisa Stinson

Walter Tackett

Maggie Wade
Albertina Walker
Irene Ware
Al Wash
The Williams Brothers
    Band
Alice Williams
Lavannah Williams
Louise Williams
Marilyn Williams
Maxie Williams
Shannon Williams
Barbara Wilson
Marvin Winans/The
    Winans
Stevie Wonder
Lin Woods
Roy Wooten
Lisa Wu-Sweat

Ron Yager

Much love and many
thanks to Donna Cromeans
for her diligent and untiring
efforts in researching all of
the initial information for
this book.

*Finally, we want to offer
special thanks to the people
who were interviewed for
this book, whose memories
have, we hope, been woven
seamlessly into the fabric of
the text.*

*Elder John Bounds
Juanita Brown
Edward Cain
Tommy Couch, Sr.
Mike Frascogna
Terrell Gatlin
Ruth Green
Ida Mae Hudson
Margie Hughes
Jerry Mannery
Rev. L.C. McCray
Josie Marie Oaties
Ray Ramsey
Bishop Donald Smith
Deliana Steward
Rosie Lee Stovall
Walter Tackett
Dennis Tobias
Theodis Westbrook
Rosie Lee White
Amanda "Mom" Williams
Huey Williams
Katrina Williams
Lavannah Williams
Marilyn Williams
Roy Wooten*

FOREWORD

> *My son, if you accept my words and
> store up my commands within you,
> turning your ear to wisdom and applying
> your heart to understanding, . . . then
> you will understand the fear of the Lord
> and find the knowledge of God.*
> Proverbs 2: 1–2, 6

Solomon declares that wisdom
and knowledge should be sought after
in order to gain insight into the beauty
of God and life.

In every one of us there should
be the desire to reach higher, to go
further, and to pursue the most ultimate
possibilities concerning our destinies.
We all have the power to do great and
wonderful things. We must first be
taught (as Solomon tried to teach his
son) that in ourselves there are dreams
and goals that are waiting to be cultivat-
ed and nurtured. Yet without God the
pursuit is in vain and is for a season.

When a child is taught that with
God all things are possible, but without
God all is lost, that child grows in the
knowledge of true love, sharing, and
caring for others as God's mandate for
living. I can truly say these characteristics
are prominent in the Williams family.

Mom and Pops have done an
excellent job of raising their children

the Lord's way. It is evident that through
their wisdom and walk with God, they
taught their children that circumstances
can change when you say, Yes I can.
Hard work and perseverance pave the
way for the future. The person who is
willing to struggle will not bow down at
the slightest degree of discomfort, but
will find another way to reach the goal.

The early morning chores and
after-school responsibilities didn't set
well with the Williams children at first,
but in hindsight these activities were the
best character builders that they could
have been given.

Now I understand why this family is
a unit of hard-working individuals who
refuse to accept no as a response to any
of life's questions. They are always ready
to find another way to reach their goals.
And you will never find a more loving
family than the Williams family.

This book should be required
reading for anyone who dares to utter
the words "I can't," "but. . . ," or
"what if it doesn't. . . ?"

Excellence is choice. You can pursue
and achieve your goals or you can sit
around and live in the realm of "what
if" for the rest of your life.

YOLANDA ADAMS CRAWFORD
Family Friend and Fan 4 Life

TABLE

OF

CONTENTS

n the Beginning: Leon and Amanda

Amanda Cain Williams sits on the pew fanning herself, waiting for the service to begin at the little country church.

The buzz of activity is increasing all around her as the sanctuary fills with people, but Mom Williams sits calmly, fanning herself with the program for Family Worship Night on this warm Sunday night in October of 1993. She feels no need to read the program; she knows what is to come.

Her boys are coming home to sing again.

The Williams Brothers have brought their gospel music sound to people from Bogue Chitto, Mississippi, to London, England; from one-room churches to a venue of millions through the magic of music television. Doug and Melvin Williams and Henry Green have received numerous awards and Grammy nominations for their songs and albums over their three-decade career. They have shared the stage with some of the greatest names in music.

This is different. This is singing for family.

They are coming home to Rose Hill Missionary Baptist Church, the little red brick building in the southern rural Mississippi community of Smithdale where their family has worshipped for decades, where generations of Williams children have sung in the choir, where their father, Leon "Pop" Williams, rests in the tiny cemetery out back, his dream realized.

Amanda smiles and nods her head slightly to herself, thinking how proud Pop would be if he were here to share in the event tonight.

In a way, she feels, he is here tonight.

Leon Williams trudged along the road to his mother's house, happy to be at the end of another day working the fields. The sun was fading a bit on the horizon but the south Mississippi humidity in rural Franklin County still hung heavy around him and mixed with the dust he kicked up as he ambled along the dirt road. Geographically, the piney woods and cotton fields he was walking past were about 30 miles north of the Mississippi-Louisiana border. Musically, they were roughly halfway between the blues of the Mississippi Delta and the jazz of New Orleans.

But Leon wasn't particularly attracted to either blues or jazz, those musical styles that had been born so close to where he grew up. Instead, he hummed a gospel tune to himself. It was the 1920s and portable radios were still a creation of the future. But no reason why he couldn't provide himself with a little traveling music, now was there? After all, young Leon loved music and there was plenty of it around the little house where he and his mother Eula lived.

Leon Williams was born in Gloster, Mississippi, on November 24, 1909, and his mother had instilled in her only son a love for gospel music and for the church. In the rural south the church had always been a powerful force, and, in small communities, the center of most lives. In the years since Reconstruction the churches that had sprung up throughout the South for black congregations had become even more important, both as spiritual centers and as hubs of political and civic leadership. And, now, in the 1920s, it seemed like Eula Williams had plans to visit every one of those churches if she could catch a ride to them.

Maybe she had turned to the church for some kind of firm foundation in her life, since she could not find much to count on in the man she had married. Leon's father wandered in and out of their lives for years and finally stopped coming back at all, until decades later when his health started to fail. But Eula had taken the responsibility for raising young Leon and his sisters and had done her best to instill in them the sense of duty and work ethic their father lacked. And she felt she had succeeded.

Nobody who knew Leon's father, Eugene Williams, was eager to confront him. They called him "Uncle Big Bud" in the south Mississippi counties of Franklin and Amite where he roamed. "That is one bad man," folks would whisper, half in awe and the other half in fear. He was powerfully built, one of those men who managed to command fearful respect without having to say a word. And he was a man who lived by only one law: his law. Big Bud made sure that no matter where he was and what he was doing, he always had his pistol with him. People in the countryside were accustomed to seeing the man trot casually past their houses on his big horse, with his pistol sticking out of the pocket of his overalls.

It was a man's world most everywhere in the early years of the 20th century, and rural black Mississippi was no exception. Big Bud had five children by Eula—a son, Leon, and four daughters, Lela, Victoria, Vernita, and Verlene—but he never allowed family obligations to interfere with his freedom to travel when and where he wished. He was rumored to have other women and other children, but anyone who questioned his activities was likely to receive a split lip from his hard hands—or worse. He was not a man to be pushed around.

Big Bud expected those under his control to understand his needs and satisfy them even before he had to voice a command. When his horse approached the big gate on the road leading to the house he and Eula shared, he had better not have to dismount to open that gate. He expected Leon or Eula or one of his daughters to hear his horse approaching and scramble out to pull the big gate wide open for him to pass through. If he had to open the gate himself, all the young people in and around the house—even visiting cousins or friends—might receive a beating. For them, the sound of Big Bud's horse had special meaning.

One often-told story is sufficient to demonstrate the stubborn—and potentially violent—nature of Eugene "Big Bud" Williams.

It was a perfect Fourth of July day for a picnic and a game of baseball, and a crowd had gathered to play on the makeshift field that had been scratched out of an expanse between tall pine trees. Everyone was having a good time, joking around and poking fun between innings, when the sound of galloping horses signaled the approach of uninvited guests. A group of white boys and men on horseback rounded the bend. The picnickers recognized several of the riders as mean-spirited rednecks, notorious for their racist attitudes, who seized every opportunity to harass black people.

It surprised no one when the horsemen trotted through the middle of the baseball field, bending down occasionally to swat one of the baseball players with the reins. The men on the ground all dodged out of the way as best they could, well knowing the consequences of fighting back. All of them, that is, but Big Bud, who had not given an inch when the horses started cutting through the baseball field. The rider who started slapping his reins at the big man who was standing his ground was in for a terrible surprise. Bud yanked his ever-present pistol from his overalls and shot at his tormentor at point-blank range. As the story goes, the shot missed only because one of Bud's friends grabbed his arm as he was pulling the trigger. The rider turned his horse and galloped away, followed by the rest of the rednecks, all cursing and screaming for revenge. The picnickers, who had stood frozen at the sound of the gunshot, stared for a moment in disbelief and then scattered through the woods. Big Bud just stood there watching the riders until they were out of sight.

The white men gathered at Homer Fenn's store, near Palmette, a small community in Amite County, to plot their revenge. "We are going to kill that nigger!" they shouted. Mr. Fenn listened to their ranting and finally offered a word of advice to the boys and men. "Well, I know the man who shot at your friend, and I've got to tell you something," Fenn said quietly. "You may kill him but some of you are going to end up dead too if you try it." But at that moment, the crowd was too furious—and too proud—to show they were paying much attention to him.

Back in Rose Hill, the tiny black community where the shooting had occurred, Big Bud had gathered his wife Eula, little Leon, and his daughters in the back room of their little house. He made them lie down on the floor while he made his plans. He tied his dog to the front gate so that anyone approaching the house would cause him to bark, sounding an alarm for those inside the house. Bud then assembled all of his firearms across the bed in the front room of the house. He quickly made sure they were all in working order and within easy reach.

Then he waited. All night long.

A few horsemen galloped back and forth past the house throughout the night, whooping and screaming threats. But none of them ever came too close to the house. Before morning, the threats had ceased. Perhaps the cool darkness calmed their tempers. More likely, they decided to heed Homer Fenn's advice.

In the months and years that followed, Big Bud moved his family around from place to place, attempting to evade those who had sworn revenge against him for the attempted shooting and for other misadventures. Eventually, when the troubling incident had faded from enough people's memories, Eugene, Eula, and their children were able to return to their home, a small cabin down the road from the farm in Smithdale, Mississippi, where Bud worked. But Big Bud continued his willful meanderings. He would disappear without a word, first for weeks, then months, returning on his horse without any explanation. The time came when he was more like a visitor to the house where Eula was raising their children.

Eula looked through the window as she stood at the stove stirring a pot of greens. She watched Leon walk toward the house. As he drew closer, she could hear the sound of his humming. She smiled and hummed along with him. Yes, she had succeeded. Leon wasn't perfect, she knew, and would no doubt sow his own wild oats and let his temper get the best of him in the future. But he never shirked his chores and he put in a solid day's work on Mr. S. A. Cain's farm without hardly a complaint. And still he had time for his music. If there was one thing Leon loved, it was his music.

She thought back to that Friday afternoon on the front porch when Leon's music had taken a whole new direction. He and his two cousins were talking and laughing. The three teenagers liked to cut up with each other when they had time to relax after a hard week of working. That afternoon, sort of out of nowhere, Leon started to sing an old hymn, "Near the Cross," that they had sung for years in church.

> *Jesus, keep me near the cross,*
> *There's a precious fountain,*
> *Free to all a healing stream*
> *Flows from Calvary's mountain.*

One cousin, W. R. Cameron, joined in with his baritone voice, then the other cousin, Augusta Anderson, added his deep, rich bass tones to the song, creating a near-perfect harmony. Eula stopped to listen. The boys kept singing, feeling the unique joy that comes from blending together in a song.

When the verse had ended, the trio sat joking for a few minutes. Then Leon spoke up. "That sounded good, boys. We ought to get us up a group."

The cousins laughed, but paid little attention to the remark, continuing their light-hearted ribbing on this lazy afternoon. A couple of hours later, Leon felt the urge to sing again. "Jesus, keep me near the cross," he sang. And again, W. R. and Augusta joined in.

"We really should get a group," Leon urged, "but we need a good tenor."

This time the other two gave the idea some serious thought. They decided to give it a try, and the search for a tenor was on. Before long, they found one in the form of another friend, A. B. Martin. They named the quartet—a gospel quartet, of course—The Big Four.

In the evenings after work, the four boys gathered at Eula's house to teach themselves new songs and how to harmonize. They worked at achieving the same sound of the gospel quartets that had become increasingly popular, groups such as The Dixie Hummingbirds, The Fairfield Four, and The Harmonizing Four.* After rehearsing for hours, they would sing for an appreciative audience of one—Leon's mother. Their repertoire consisted of just a few songs, but their sound was pleasant, enough so that Eula planned to take The Big Four out with her on weekend "missionary trips."

Eula possessed one of the deepest Christian faiths Leon had ever known. For as long as he could remember, he had accompanied her as she spread the teachings of Jesus in small Missionary Baptist churches throughout the state, wherever they would have her.

It wasn't always easy to make the weekend trips from church to church. When they didn't travel in one of their own cars or couldn't hitch a ride with someone going their way, the Big Four—and Eula—would walk the long dusty roads, singing all the way.

---

* *These three groups are still going strong, though most of the original members are deceased. The Dixie Hummingbirds, based in Philadelphia, Pennsylvania and the Harmonizing Four, from Richmond, Virginia, go back to the 1930s, and the Fairfield Four, based in Nashville, Tennessee, were founded in 1921.*

There were no strangers in the world of the The Big Four. If they had to stay the night, the boys and Eula Williams were welcome in the homes of congregation members. Often they delighted their hosts with a sneak preview of their upcoming performances.

It was the mid-1920s, and the world was almost two decades away from the first commercial television broadcasts. One of the chief sources of entertainment and fellowship in black communities was the staging of gospel music performances and competitions. After a six-day week of following the mule down row after row or chopping wood in the blistering Mississippi sun, the country folk would load up a wagon or simply set out on foot for the nearest church where the singings might be held.

The day came when the group heard that a contest for gospel quartets was going to take place at a church near enough for them to get to. Leon, W.R., Augusta, and A.B. began practicing. They practiced until they were nearly too hoarse to sing. They had something to prove. They believed they were just as good as the professional quartets. Most of their competition had been coached by professionals and were already earning some type of living by singing on a circuit. The Big Four, on the other hand, usually sang for the sheer joy of offering their musical gifts to the Lord. While the other groups could afford lessons from an experienced quartet singer, The Big Four relied on their instincts and their talent.

The day for the contest arrived. The four boys fought back the jitters as they stood before the judges. But the familiar song they had chosen for the competition helped soothe their nerves and calm their fears.

> *Jesus, keep me near the cross,*
> *There's a precious fountain,*
> *Free to all a healing stream*
> *Flows from Calvary's mountain.*

The Big Four won the contest. It was the fledgling group's proudest moment. Leon would remember throughout his life the three happy years of singing with his cousins and his friend, a partnership that dissolved only when W. R. got married and moved away.

Leon never lost his love for gospel music. By the time The Big Four split up, his foundation was firmly planted in the church and he found plenty of opportunities to sing in the choir there. On weekdays, he worked from dawn to dusk doing farm work. And, like most young men, he began to think of building a family.

The farm where Eula and her five children worked and lived was owned by S. A. and Josephine Cain, God-fearing people who worked hard and raised ten children. The Williams cabin was close to the main farmhouse, and Leon got to know the family well.

The grueling schedule of working the farm combined with the rigors of raising the children took its toll on Josephine Cain, who had been sickly most of her life anyway. By the time she was 30, her health was so poor that the care of the younger children fell to her two oldest daughters, Mafalda and Amanda.

It was 13-year-old Amanda who caught the eye of 23-year-old Leon.

The responsibilities of taking care of her younger siblings had made Amanda mature beyond her years. Leon had seen the shy girl around the farm and had spoken to her politely in passing from time to time. They got to know each other better when they began singing together in the choir at Rose Hill Church.

The soft-spoken Amanda had noticed Leon as well. She knew about him from his days with the Big Four and loved the way he sang, but she didn't really get to know him until the choir rehearsals at the church.

It wasn't long before Leon started coming to the Cain farm, to ask Amanda if he could walk her to rehearsal. Amanda agreed eagerly. She loved spending time with Leon, and hearing his deep, infectious laugh could always make her feel better. Soon there were more walks, long talks, and occasionally Leon would join Amanda and her family for Sunday dinner.

The couple courted this way for nearly two years.

One night in late December 1934, they were strolling along the path that led home from the church. Choir practice had gone well. Without preamble, Leon turned to Amanda and asked, "How about it, why don't we get married?"

Amanda looked at him for a moment, hesitating. It was an age when girls often married quite young, but she still had many responsibilities at home. But this was a man, a good man, a man she could love always.

The pause was brief, as was her answer.

"Okay," Amanda said.

Her acceptance of his proposal wasn't the final hurdle, however. Leon was still a young man, but his mother had raised him to always make sure he did the right thing in every situation, as best as he could determine. What he did next would forever endear him to Amanda and to her family. When the pair reached her house, Leon asked to excuse himself in order to speak to her father. Amanda and her mother waited eagerly in the kitchen while Leon formally asked S.A. for his daughter's hand in marriage.

Leon's love and sincerity were obvious to Amanda's father, and he knew the boy was a hard worker, as evidenced by the excellent condition of the farm he worked. Mr. Cain knew this young man would be a good husband to his daughter. He gave his permission.

Not one to waste time, Leon displayed one of the traits that would mark him for life—the ability to make a quick decision. He set the wedding for the next day, which was New Year's Eve, 1934. What better way to ring in the New Year, he thought, than with a wedding?

That night Amanda was beset by doubts. It had all happened so fast. Leon had been her one and only boyfriend. And even though she was 15, an age at which many girls in the rural south got married, she still wondered if she might be too young to get married. But she thought it through, and had a long talk with herself. By morning, her mind was at peace. Marrying Leon was right.

She pulled her best dress from her closet. It was blue, her favorite color, and had a flowing skirt. Her older sister Mafalda had agreed to go along and be her maid of honor.

Soon Leon, wearing his pale gray suit, arrived in his mule-drawn wagon. Amanda and her sister climbed in the back, careful not to get their clothes dirty. Riding there with them was their father's close friend Dallas Weatherspoon, who was going to be a witness. Leon and his soon-to-be father-in-law sat up front and drove the mule on a bumpy 20-mile ride into the small town of Bude, Mississippi.

By the time they made it to town, almost everything had closed early for New Year's Eve. There wasn't a Justice of the Peace to be found. After a frantic search, a minister was located and at exactly 4 p.m. Leon and Amanda became husband and wife. Years later, Amanda still sometimes wondered why this caring, devoted man had chosen her, a young girl. Finally, she asked Leon. He said simply, "I wanted to get you before someone else did."

CHAPTER II

Hoeing a Hard Row:
Raising a Family

Amanda smiles and nods as the church continues to fill with people. Seems everyone from all around the area has heard about The Williams Brothers singing here tonight.

Sitting next to her in a stylish white suit is her youngest daughter Marilyn, and next to her, with her perennial smile, is middle daughter Josie Marie. In the pew in front of them is her oldest daughter Deliana. Amanda watches Deliana give a quick smile and nod of encouragement to her two grown daughters Amanda and Linder, who are sitting quietly with the choir.

Other family members are spread throughout the small sanctuary—grandchildren and cousins and nieces and nephews and aunts and uncles—all sharing in the celebration and worship time tonight.

The excitement had been building long before anyone got to the church. All day long,

Amanda's phone rang with calls from people telling her how much they were looking forward to the service that night.

As the choir starts to sing, Mom Williams closes her eyes and lets the music flow over her. She has been coming to Rose Hill Church ever since she was a child. It is especially gratifying that so many of her family can be here for this special night. The audience sways with the harmony of the choir as they praise the Lord, raising their voices with all the strength and emotion they have.

The newlyweds started from scratch.

Amanda moved in with Leon and his mother, sharing the small house— a cabin, really—on the farm her grandfather had built. On the next hill over, she could see her father's house. Almost all the newlyweds' worldly goods were out back in the barn: a mule, a horse, and a hog. The few chickens they had wandered loose in the yard.

The house had no electricity. The family ate their evening meals, cooked on an old wood stove, by the light of kerosene lamps. After dinner, Leon would bring out the family's battery-operated radio and the couple would listen and sing along with whatever gospel radio programs they could tune in. When it came time to turn in, they would cuddle together on freshly washed linens. Amanda took great pride in washing and ironing the few items they had. Carefully folded on the foot of the bed was one of the quilts Eula had made for them as a wedding present.

The first year was especially hard for Amanda. Her mother's sickness grew progressively worse, and just three months after she and Leon were married, Josephine Bell Cain died.

While many women would consider it a burden to live with their mother-in-law, Amanda found it a blessing. Eula became a surrogate mother to her, even as she mourned the death of her own mother. In addition to being a friend and companion, Eula taught her young daughter-in-law to cook a number of new dishes, and how to hone her skills at mending and sewing.

Leon had goals. He wanted to buy more livestock (during their second year of marriage he bought two milk cows), and he wanted to save enough money to buy a place of their own. But that didn't mean he neglected to give Amanda a surprise gift from time to time. When he had put enough money aside, he liked to go into town and pick her out a new dress. His young bride was surprised at how quickly he learned her preferences, always picking out just the right size and color.

People throughout America were suffering from deprivation caused by the Great Depression. For the rural folk of southern Mississippi, who were accustomed to scratching out a living from the soil, life didn't change all that much. Hard work was the norm, and it was no different for Leon and Amanda. The young couple settled into a regular routine of long workdays and peaceful evenings.

Amanda got up every morning just before sunrise to make biscuits, gravy, and bacon for breakfast. She took a bucket down to the barn to milk one of the cows so they could have fresh milk in their coffee.

Then it was off to the fields to work. Amanda and Leon worked the fields together, and their chores were never the same from one day to the next. One day they might saw fence posts together, on the next day dig ditches, then on another hoe rows of cotton, corn, peanuts, potatoes, or whatever else they were growing. And, of course, there was the plowing.

Amanda had been plowing behind a mule for more than half her life and she wasn't about to stop now. Her father had taught her how to plow when she was seven. He would set her off in a row and she would take off by herself. When the plow hit a root and got stuck, Amanda wasn't big enough or strong enough to pull it out by herself, so she had to sit and wait for her father before she could start again. Amanda loved plowing. There was something deeply satisfying about looking back and seeing the fresh earth uncovered in a long furrow behind her.

Amanda and Leon worked the fields until around noon and then went back to the house to have lunch with Eula. After lunch it was back to the fields until 5:30 or 6 in the evening. That was the routine six days a week. The Scriptures said the seventh day was to be a day of rest. To Amanda and Leon, that meant taking a day of rest from the world's work. Sunday was a day to do the Lord's work. Early on Sunday mornings, the two would travel with Eula and become part of her continuing missionary work for Rose Hill Missionary Baptist Church.

All of the hard work on the farm paid off with a good cotton crop that first year. Amanda and Leon knew exactly what to do with the money they earned from selling that crop.

They bought furniture. At the top of their shopping list was a new wood-burning stove, a chifforobe, and not one but two beds. They were going to need the extra bed later in the year. Leon and Amanda were about to face another challenge together—parenthood—just eleven months after they were married.

The thought of being a mother did not concern Amanda that much, even at the young age of 16. After all, she'd had lots of practice with babies. She had taken care of her younger brothers and sisters during her mother's long illness.

On the night of November 12, 1935, she and Leon and Eula were gathered around the dinner table listening to the radio at 8 p.m. Amanda hadn't been paying much attention to the preaching that had been pouring from the radio's tinny speakers. She was too busy counting contractions.

The time-honored routines of country midwifery swung into action. Eula took over and sent Leon off to fetch Mrs. Sarah Martin, the community midwife. A flustered Leon came back soon with Mrs. Martin in tow. The two older women took Amanda into the bedroom and made her comfortable. Leon was banished from the room. He took up his nervous pacing from the kitchen into the living room and back into the kitchen again, stopping occasionally to put an ear to the door of the bedroom.

Three hours later, just before midnight, Leon Williams, Jr., later nicknamed "Bill," was born.

A little more than a year later, on January 29, 1937, Bill was joined by a baby sister. Eula took one look at her new granddaughter, an adorable little girl with a full head of black curly hair, and named her Shirley Temple Williams after her favorite movie star. Leon Williams would have none of that, however, and immediately changed the baby's name to Deliana (now mostly called by one of two nicknames, "Granny" or "Tee")

From 1937 to 1949, the Williamses had occasion to call on the local midwife four more times. Huey was born on September 21, 1938, Josie Marie (nicknamed "Ree") on July 14, 1942, and Frank on June 25, 1947. All three, like Leon Jr. and Tee, were born in the front bedroom of the house. Sadly, their sixth child, Douglas MacArthur, died just 21 days after his birth in June of 1949.

Amanda stepped away from the stove where her husband's noontime meal was waiting for him. She had heard Leon's boots clump up the steps and across the porch but he was nowhere to be found in the small house. Amanda heard the hammering from across the yard where a new house was slowly taking shape. She knew just where to look for Leon. Walking past her babies playing on the floor she peered through the window. There he was, up on the roof, asking questions, taking a hammer, and pounding the roofing shingles onto the decking. Amanda smiled and shook her head. Leon was working as hard on this house as he did on everything else.

Less than a year ago, in January 1938, Amanda and Leon and their two children had moved out of Eula's small house. When Amanda's widowed father decided to leave Smithdale, the couple moved into the house that Amanda had grown up in, giving the young mother what she considered the perfect place to start raising her children. She hadn't realized how big Leon's dreams were at that time.

Leon Williams had grown up not owning much at all except the clothes on his back, and though his mother had done her best to provide for him, he wanted more for his children. He didn't want to depend on anyone else in any way if he could help it. He had worked other people's land, bringing in the cotton crop and paying the landowner for the right to do so. He dreamed of having a farm of his own; that way, he thought, he would be rewarded for every bit of his labor, producing rewards for his family to enjoy. Just down the road from the Cain farmhouse was a 100-acre plot of land owned by a man by the name of Dan Thornton. Leon had had his eye on that land for a while, and he knew that Mr. Thornton really wasn't doing much with it. The problem was coming up with the money to buy the property.

One day, Mr. Thornton saw Leon out in the fields and stopped to talk to him. "Leon, wouldn't you like to buy this property?" Mr. Thornton asked, waving his arm in the direction of the 100 acres he owned. "Well, I surely would, Mr. Thornton," Leon said, "but I just don't have the money for that right now."

Thornton then told the younger man about a federal program through which hard-working people who qualified could borrow the money to buy land. "Do you have a wagon and a mule?" Thornton asked Leon, who nodded. "Well, then, I believe you would qualify for the program." A few days later, Thornton took Leon in his car to Meadville, the seat of Franklin County, to complete the paperwork.

A few months later, Leon and Amanda finally were able to make an offer on that 100-acre plot. Mr. Thornton accepted and that land was to become the home for the Williams family from that time forward.

There was already a structure on the Thornton property, and though it wasn't exactly what Amanda had in mind, she had been through too much hardship in her young life to question its suitability. Leon, Amanda, Eula, and the two toddlers moved into the five-room, wood-frame house. A long porch surrounded the house, and there were three tiny bedrooms and a catwalk. Amanda's pride and joy was her large kitchen where she cooked meals on an old wood stove. One thing the house didn't have was electricity. A warm flickering light was provided by kerosene lamps.

Even though the Depression had slowed the country's economy to the point that virtually no houses were being constructed, Leon dreamed of building his own house. One of the many New Deal programs in place at the time was a federal loan program through which first-time home builders could receive assistance. Leon applied and was accepted. Before long, workmen and craftsmen were hard at work on the first and only house that he and Amanda would own together. And Leon insisted on helping build it. Whenever he had an extra minute, he would pester the workmen to let him lend a hand. Besides, he thought, there was always something new to learn, wasn't there? He paid particular attention to the brick masons who were constructing the chimney for the fireplace. He had always thought he could learn that trade. And, eventually, he did learn it.

In 1941, Leon, Amanda, Eula, and the first three children—Bill, Deliana, and Huey—moved into their new home. The Big House, as it would later come to be known, stood close to the dirt road that ran alongside their property and was surrounded by pine trees and fertile ground. In 1942, Josie Marie was born, but it was 1943 before they got electricity.

CHAPTER III

Williams Family Singers

People are swaying to the music of the choir at Rose Hill Missionary Baptist Church.
An "Amen'" or a "Hallelujah!" punctuates the rhythm of the song as it rolls over the
crowded room.

Amanda closes her eyes as she listens, just as she has done for so many years here in
her church. Mom Williams is known here.

Her namesake granddaughter Amanda steps down from the choir loft to sing a solo.
As she takes the microphone in her hand and begins to sing, the crowd stirs and leans
forward. This is the daughter of Deliana, the first daughter and second child of Leon and
Amanda Williams. The emotion of the evening, however, proves to be too much for young
Amanda. Her voice cracks with hoarseness and falters as the choir continues singing in the
background. Mom Williams feels her eyes moisten for the beautiful young lady she sees
struggling to regain her voice.

Amanda's sister Linder comes down from the choir and puts her arm around Amanda's shoulders. At the same moment, another choir soloist steps forward and, even though she has never sung this music before, takes up the song where young Amanda left off. The sisters stand close by, their arms around each other, and whisper the lyrics to the soloist who lifts her voice in a song she has never sung before.

The Spirit of the Lord is moving here tonight as the evening builds toward the special music to come.

There was one thing all the Williams children learned from their earliest years: how to work. And Leon didn't just talk about it. He set the example.

He worked that 100 acres from top to bottom, raising food for his family but also growing cotton and a "truck patch" of various crops for sale: peppers, sweet potatoes, Irish potatoes, peanuts, sweet corn, butterbeans, string beans, watermelon, and okra. At various times, he grew sugarcane and even set up a mule-driven press to make syrup from the cane.

If Pop saw the opportunity to do something to make money to support his family, he launched into the venture full force. He ran across a deal on some cobbling equipment and taught himself to make and repair shoes. That same thing happened with blacksmith equipment, and soon people around the countryside were calling on him to perform blacksmithing chores for their animals. Whenever he ran across a trade that interested him, whether it was barbering or automobile mechanics, he would learn enough to master it, then offer his services to his family and to others.

The farm was almost entirely self-sustaining. If Amanda needed cornmeal, then fresh corn was taken from the field to the local store in Smithdale where it was ground into meal. Vegetables came from the garden and the meat came from killing hogs. They would hang up the hog, strip and clean it, cut the choice meats, and grind sausage, all under the big tree next to the house. Leon even built his own smokehouse for smoking meat. He would salt the meat, let it sit for a few days, dip it in hot water, then in cold water. He would then take wire or hangers and string slabs of bacon and sausage across the racks, letting them smoke for two weeks. A hog killing was a big event in a rural community. Neighbors would come help with the preparation of the meat, earning a portion of it to carry home with them. When their time came to kill a hog, the favor was returned. Hams, ribs, chops, chitterlings, and various other parts of the hog's anatomy were enjoyed for a long time to come after each event.

All of the children learned the chores of the farm and were assigned duties as soon as they grew big enough to handle them. Milking the cows meant getting up before dawn and stumbling out to the field to herd the cows back to the barn (each child had a specific group of cows as his or her responsibility), milk them, then carry the milk buckets back to the house, all before breakfast. In the afternoons after school, work in the fields beckoned. Every Williams child knew the feel of bruised fingertips from plucking the cotton bolls and the heavy weight of a six-foot sack of cotton being dragged down the rows of cotton after hours of back-bending labor. When enough cotton was picked to make a bale, it was loaded on a wagon behind Pop's old tractor and driven five miles down the road to the cotton gin in Smithdale. There was always work to be done, and the Williams family learned the lessons early of reaping what they sowed and doing it together.

The family lived far enough out in the country that Smithdale was considered "town" even though it consisted only of a general store, a post office, a hardware store, a cotton gin, and a welding shop. Anything that couldn't be home-grown or home-made could be bought at one of the stores: nails and hammers and other tools, or salt for canning or curing meat. And, of course, on special occasions, a cold soda pop would make for the perfect ending to a hot day in the sun.

Leon's abilities weren't confined to work on the farm. He taught himself carpentry and brick masonry, and eventually became an independent brick contractor. Contractors who needed brickwork soon learned they could count on Leon Williams' crews. All the Williams boys learned how to lay brick. They started when they were so little the only thing they could do was carry a few bricks to their father, then advanced to mixing mortar and the actual bricklaying itself. All those efforts paid off as the boys earned spending money during summer vacation by laying brick with their dad's crews.

Sometimes, Leon's work during the year would take him away from home for days and weeks at a time. Without fail he would appear at the end of a job with pockets full of treats for his children.

Leon was always ready with his booming laugh at the first sign of humor, but the children knew when to take him seriously. Farm life was hard and everyone knew that the chores were to be done and done well. Pop's huge hands were as hard as the bricks he handled all day long. The feel of one of them as the deliverer of discipline was not an experience a Williams child wanted to endure often.

Throughout his life, Leon worked to instill in his children certain interrelated precepts he considered to be the foundations of success. One was "Have Your Own." That meant not depending on other people to take care of you, but having your own means for providing for yourself and your family. The way to have your own was to work hard and exercise what Leon referred to as "staying power." He would often remind them that "It's not how you start, it's how you finish."

It wasn't easy street for a black family out in the boondocks of Mississippi, especially during the low times of the Great Depression. They had few luxuries but they learned how to do a lot with a little. Most of all, they had each other. And they had their music.

Leon took seriously his responsibility to care for his family's needs; it drove him to work long hours. Yet in spite of the demands of his work schedule, his love for gospel music remained as strong as ever.

Leon and Amanda still sang in the choir at Rose Hill, as did the children when they grew old enough to carry a tune. In addition, the young couple formed a gospel singing group called The Southern Gospel Singers, which included cousins and friends who loved to bring special music to churches in the area. Meanwhile, the Williams children were hanging on every note during the group's rehearsals at the church.

One day, Leon Jr., Deliana, and one of their cousins were outside in the yard playing church while the adults socialized inside. The youngsters, no older than seven or eight, mimicked the preacher, then grouped together to sing. What lyrics they couldn't remember, they made up on the spot. The young voices got louder and louder until the adults inside the house stopped their conversation.

"Those kids sound pretty good," said Leon. Just by the sound of his voice Amanda knew that an idea was being hatched inside her husband's head. She also knew there was no turning away when Pop Williams started "growing a plan."

Pop formed a children's gospel singing group called The Southern Gospel Juniors. At first the group consisted of Bill and Deliana and some of the cousins. Leon carted them to church services, revivals, and any other meeting where they could sing. Coached by Leon, the children practiced in the evenings after school, learning new songs and how to harmonize. No workday was strenuous enough for Pop to cancel one of those evening practice sessions.

When the littler children were old enough, they became part of The Southern Gospel Singers—first Huey, then Josie Marie, then Frank. Until 1954, when she married and moved away, Deliana acted as the group's "mother," traveling with them to take care of details. When Deliana left, Josie Marie, an accomplished soloist herself, took up her sister's duties as the unofficial road manager. In about 1960 The Southern Gospel Juniors became a boys' gospel group, but Josie Marie stayed on as manager, guiding them from one meeting to another as they pleased congregations throughout southern Mississippi and Louisiana with their sweet voices and tight harmony.

The traveling made for short nights on occasion. Many a weekend the boys would arrive home from a concert at 2 a.m., only to be expected to rise at 6 to tend the mules or cows. One memorable Monday morning, Huey and Josie Marie leaned against a tree, just for a short rest between morning chores. Later that morning, the others found them fast asleep, sitting straight up, and roused them just in time to leave for school.

Amanda Williams gave birth to children over a period of 21 years—from 1935 to 1956—so there were basically two groups of children. In the first group, all born during the forties and all born at home in Smithdale, were Leon Jr., Deliana, Huey, Josie Marie, and Frank. In the second group, all of whom were born at Charity Hospital in Natchez, about 45 minutes from Smithdale, were the children of the fifties: Leonard (July 1, 1951), Melvin (July 21, 1953), Marilyn (October 8, 1954), and Doug (September 3, 1956).

However dedicated to their music and their chores, the children, from both groups, were not beyond temptation when it came to the call for mischief. Like all children, they teased and played tricks on one another with abandon. When Josie Marie was about six years old, Bill and Huey told her about the millions of bats that lived in the woods that would chase her if she walked out there alone. She put on a brave front and proclaimed how she didn't believe them a bit. One evening, she was walking back from the barn and thought she felt the whoosh of wings close by her head. Zoom. She went running back to the house, arms flailing and her screams mixing with the gales of laughter from her brothers.

Many memories of the children's earliest years come from Inez and L. S. Jackson, next-door neighbors to the Williamses from 1951 on. Almost as soon as she moved in, Inez—who is known as Aunt Nez by the whole family—became unofficial godmother to all the Williams children who had already been born, and she continued to fill that role for the ones who came along later. Her help—which included creating countless fabulous meals for the entire clan, without benefit of a single recipe—was indispensable to Amanda.

One of Aunt Nez's fondest recollections is of a trick *she* played on Doug and his niece Amanda, probably some time in 1959. Doug and Amanda (the oldest child of Deliana and Willie Banks), who were about the same age, were pestering Aunt Nez relentlessly. Aunt Nez, who had no misgivings about doling out punishment when the occasion called for it, told them, "You kids better stop bothering me or I'm going to hang you up in that tree in a croker sack!" The children giggled and kept annoying their favorite neighbor while she sat calmly fanning herself on the porch. After a while, the two young ones conked out on the porch, sleeping as only preschoolers can. They woke up, inside the sack, to the sound of Aunt Nez's cackling. Having made good on her threat, she let them kick and holler for just a bit before letting them out.

A couple of years later, five-year-old Doug was watching his brothers play "baseball" with wasps in the yard. The rules were simple. Leonard and Melvin would throw a rock at a wasp nest, then take a stick and bat the wasps away as they came near. If the cloud of wasps grew too ominous, it was time to practice their running skills. Little Doug, after observing this exhilarating game for weeks, decided to sneak out one afternoon and try his skills at waspball. He got the first part of the game right, as the rock he threw definitely stirred up the wasps. His coordination was not up to his older brothers' level yet, however, and when the wasps surrounded him, they immediately zeroed in on his little bald head. His young legs carried him back to the house as fast as they could go, where his mother applied tobacco to the dozen or so trophy bumps the wasps had delivered to his noggin.

As the youngest child, Doug sometimes drew the ire of the brothers closest to him, Melvin and Leonard. "Doug was Mama's pet, no doubt about it," remembers Melvin with a laugh. "Of course, we took every opportunity to pick on him. He used to only like the breast pieces of the chicken, so Leonard and I would make sure to get the breast pieces off the platter of fried chicken so Doug would have to eat a leg or something.

"And we thought he would always get away with playing sick, especially when it came time to go to the garden and work. One day, he was saying he had a headache and he wasn't doing any work in the garden. He was always tall and skinny so we could throw him around. We told him, 'You are lying; ain't nothing wrong with you. Get over it and get to work.' He said we couldn't tell him what to do. So we said, 'If you're not gonna work, then you are going to eat dirt,' and I grabbed him and pushed his face down in the peanut patch where we were digging up the leftover peanuts after it had rained.

"Doug started grabbing for a dirt clod to throw at me, so I ran away laughing, out to a safe-enough distance to dodge the dirt Doug was throwing. He was mad. I turned my head and when I turned back I saw this brick bat flying at me. It hit me right under my eye and I ran back to the house crying about how Doug had hit me. Mama said, 'Well, you shouldn't have been pushing his head into the dirt.'

"After that, we were a little more cautious of Doug."

1944–1972

OVERLEAF: *By the mid-1960s, when this photograph was taken, Pop Williams had been organizing groups of gospel singers for over two decades: The Southern Gospel Singers in the 1940s and 1950s, The Southern Gospel Juniors in the 1950s, and The Little Williams Brothers in the early 1960s. Taken in Henry Green's living room, this is the oldest existing shot of any of The Williams Brothers groupings. Top row, left to right: Leonard Williams, Henry Green, Doug Bell (a cousin on Amanda's side of the family); bottom row, left to right: Thomas T. Barnes (a family friend from Smithdale), Doug Williams, Melvin Williams.*

TOP: *Samuel Alfred Cain, Amanda Cain's father.*

ABOVE, LEFT: *Leon "Pop" Williams in 1944.*

ABOVE, RIGHT: *Amanda Williams in 1949.*

LEFT: *Deliana, the oldest of the girls, in a studio shot taken in the early 1950s. Deliana sang with The Southern Gospel Singers and also became their unofficial road manager.*

RIGHT: *Leon "Bill" Williams, Jr., the oldest of the Williams children. This picture was taken some time in the late 1940s.*

BELOW: *Josie Marie in 1953, leaning on Pop's car in front of the big house. After Deliana moved away from Smithdale, Marie became the "mother" of The Southern Gospel Singers, staying with them even after they became a boys-only group, in 1960.*

ABOVE: *Huey Williams at nineteen. (In the foreground is baby Amanda Banks, Deliana and Willie's first child, born in May of 1956.) Huey has sung with various groups during his musical career, including The Southern Gospel Singers, Henry Harris and the Flying Clouds (from Detroit), and The Jackson Southernaires.*

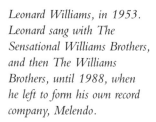

Leonard Williams, in 1953. Leonard sang with The Sensational Williams Brothers, and then The Williams Brothers, until 1988, when he left to form his own record company, Melendo.

Frank Williams, probably about 1960. Frank sang on a few occasions with The Little Williams Brothers and many years with The Jackson Southernaires, but is best remembered as the founder of the world-famous Mississippi Mass Choir. Frank died in 1993.

ABOVE, LEFT: *Melvin Williams, in the early 1960s. Melvin, who has sung with Williams Brothers groups since he was a little boy, is a multitalented musician-songwriter, vocalist, genius in the studio. He also co-founded Melendo Music Publishing and Blackberry Records.*

ABOVE, CENTER: *Marilyn Williams, born in 1954, has been an integral part of The Williams Brothers success: as secretary for The Sensational Williams Brothers, secretary/ receptionist for Blackberry Entertainment, and executive administrative assistant for Blackberry Records. She is now vice-president of operations of Blackberry Records.*

ABOVE, RIGHT: *Three-year-old Doug Williams, shown here on Christmas with his toy phone, did his first lead solo for The Little Williams Brothers when he was five. CEO of Blackberry Records, Doug is known for his ability to focus on goals, both for The Williams Brothers music ministry and for the record label.*

A 1968 shot of (clockwise from top left) Leonard Williams, Henry Green, Doug Williams, and Melvin Williams, who sang together for the next two decades. The group is inside radio station WAPF in McComb, Mississippi.

CHAPTER IV

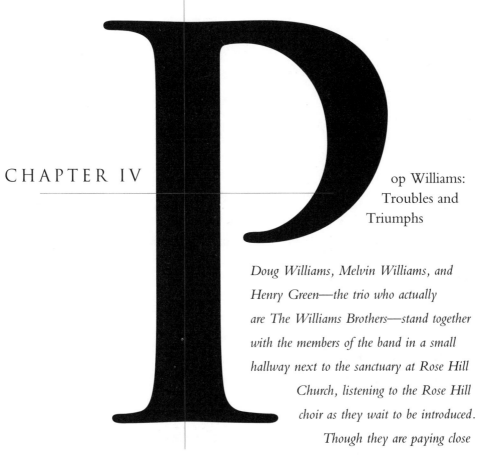

Pop Williams:
Troubles and
Triumphs

*Doug Williams, Melvin Williams, and
Henry Green—the trio who actually
are The Williams Brothers—stand together
with the members of the band in a small
hallway next to the sanctuary at Rose Hill
Church, listening to the Rose Hill
choir as they wait to be introduced.
Though they are paying close
attention to the music, all three can't help but let their thoughts wander as they wait. Not
surprisingly, they all are remembering Pop.*

*Henry smiles as he remembers how Pop first came to hear him sing as a young man
at his church in nearby Liberty. "You need to come sing with us, son," Pop had said after
church that day, never one to beat around the bush.*

*Melvin chuckles to himself as he recalls Pop's boisterous laugh whenever anything
tickled his fancy. You could hear that laugh a mile away, and it was difficult not to join in,
even if the joke was on you.*

*Doug thinks about his earliest memories of Pop, how he would seem so gruff at times,
but would always seem ready to lend the right word or a helping hand when the situation
called for it.*

Pop Williams wasn't a troublemaker. Everyone knew that. Sure he had a temper at times, but his reputation as a hard worker and a craftsman who delivered quality work was well-known throughout the surrounding counties of Smithdale.

Then what was he doing in jail?

Little Doug looked up at the window on the second floor with the bars across it. It was so strange to be visiting his father at a place like this that it was . . . well . . . it was fascinating. He looked up at his mother, who walked beside him with the basket of food for Pop. Oh well, it was only for a few more days.

Leon's brief stay in jail was almost a comedy of errors, except that it reminded him of the injustice of the times. He was no crusader for civil rights; he was too busy working to spend time waving banners. But, why, he wondered, couldn't a man be treated like a man? Leon smiled as he watched his wife and youngest son walk toward the jail. Another lesson in patience for him from the Lord, he reckoned.

He had known about racism all his life, but he had accepted it as part of the society in which he operated. His way of overcoming it had been to work hard to put food on his family's table, clothes on their backs, and a roof over their heads. He figured that the Lord would provide for him if he did his part. That didn't mean the Lord was finished molding Leon's character yet. He was a strong man with a strong opinion about how things should be in most cases. Sometimes that caused a little bit of ruckus in his life.

Leon had been hungry after working hard on a job site all morning. He hadn't had time to bring food with him that morning, and by the time the noon break rolled around, he was ravenous. He remembered that a small drive-in diner was close to the house he was laying the brick for. He pulled up to the diner, got out of his truck, and walked up to the window where no other customer was waiting to be served.

"I would like a hamburger, please," Leon told the man behind the counter.

"You have to go around to the back for that," the man told him.

Leon felt more irritation than real anger. It wasn't the first time he had been sent to a back door with a sign that said, "Colored People Entrance." But today he was tired of it. "I'll just go somewhere else," Leon answered and spun on his heel and walked back to his truck. He revved the motor a little too much as he pulled out of the gravel driveway of the diner, sending a few rocks flying as he spun off. Leon didn't look around as he drove way, so didn't know until the police showed up at his job site the next day that one of those rocks had shattered a window in the diner. Before arresting him, the cop told Leon that if he didn't like the way things were done down South, he could move up North.

Now, here he was, on a trumped-up charge, spending seven days in a dank jail with people who had intentionally broken the law. He smiled at his wife as she handed him a home-cooked meal through the bars. He looked down at his son. "It's okay, boy."

And Doug knew that if his Pop said it was okay, it was. Everything would be fine.

During that week in jail, Leon's thoughts inevitably turned to another, darker time in his life, before he married Amanda, started working his own land, and raising a family. Though Eula had done her best to instill in all her children the teachings of the Bible, it was difficult to live up to those high standards day in and day out. Leon had yet to learn some hard, sorrowful lessons, lessons only experience can teach.

Like many hard-working young men in rural, pre-Depression America, Leon had allowed himself a routine consisting of working in the fields during the week, followed by a weekend reward of partying. On one of those party weekends, a combination of alcohol and anger (a deadly mix he would warn his children about in the decades ahead) almost led to his downfall. Leon regarded it as the closest he ever came to following the path taken by his errant father, Eugene "Big Bud" Williams.

It was at a house party one night in the late 1920s that Leon came face to face with the worst in himself. He had been drinking and enjoying the music, dancing and joking, his infectious laugh filling the room. Everyone was having a good time, and Leon joined in with all the enthusiasm that was in his nature. He was dancing with a woman when suddenly he felt a rough hand on his shoulder. A man had grabbed him and was angrily accusing him of trying to steal his woman.

Leon reeled backwards. He was grappling with his attacker when he saw a flash of steel and felt a knife stabbing down his shoulder and side. As the two wrestled, a loud "Boom!" reverberated through the room. The man fell. Leon looked down at his hand, which held a smoking pistol, a weapon he, like most black men in the south, usually carried.

The man Leon shot did not recover, and though the courts ruled that Leon had acted in self-defense, the dead man's family and friends swore revenge. Leon, though he felt guilty and despondent, knew that he must do whatever he could to protect the family. He moved Eula and his siblings to the next county, and even changed his name for a while. It was months before Leon decided that it was safe to return to Smithdale.

Though Pop Williams rarely talked about the incident in the years to come, it caused him to suffer many a sleepless night. And for a long time he was haunted by nightmares that jolted him awake, screaming and in a delirious sweat. On those nights, Amanda would hold him, trying with the warmth of her touch and comforting words to show him that he could truly forgive himself for that long-ago mistake. Eventually, the nightmares ceased, but Leon's closest friends knew that the memory of that fatal error in judgment was always with him.

The tragedy and its aftermath might have completely crushed the spirit of many men. For Leon, however, the memory served as a constant reminder of the dangers of bad company and too much freedom. He promised himself that when he had children of his own he would do everything in his power to keep them from falling into the same traps he had.

And he kept that promise.

Only God knows how much that single event had to do with the later direction of Leon's life. Maybe it shook him up so much that he vowed to focus all his energies on supporting and developing the potential of his family. The evidence of his life seems to indicate that was the case. And the proof is in the character of the children he and Amanda raised. None of their children ever got into trouble with the law—or with anyone else, for that matter. They knew that if they ever brought any trouble on themselves, they would have to answer to their father. Other kids they knew might be allowed to run wild with little or no supervision. But the Williams family was ever under the watchful eyes of Leon and Amanda.

Some might have said it was a case of "do as I say, not as I do" for Leon. After all, in the split second it had taken for the bullet from Leon's gun to fly a few feet, another man's life had been snuffed out, and his own nearly destroyed. Yet he refused to allow his children even to approach the edges of bad influence. Not a man to think he had to explain his motives to many people, Pop Williams probably would have shrugged at that line of reasoning. He had suffered for his awful mistake. It couldn't be undone, he might say. But if any good could come out of what he had done, his children—and others—would receive that goodness. So whatever anyone might say, his mistake would benefit his children. He and Amanda would do everything in their power to keep the children from coming anywhere near that kind of mistake.

Leon developed a combination of street-smarts and business savvy uncommon for a black man who had grown up in rural Mississippi and who had ended his formal education when he finished eighth grade. Though his anger still flashed from time to time, he managed to corral it enough to accomplish the goals he had set. Over the years, many would comment on Pop Williams' ability to handle an enormous physical workload, whether it was working the farm or laying brick or building a house, all the while dealing with concert promoters and lawyers and record company executives over every detail that would affect his singing groups.

And yet his family and neighbors around the Smithdale community knew him as a person willing to help anyone with a need. He brought one of his sisters (and her children) into his home when they needed a place to stay during a troubled period. When his own father developed health problems in later years, Leon and Amanda cared for Eugene in their home until his death in 1951. If he were visiting with a friend whose wagon or automobile needed repairing, Leon would pitch in and do what he could to help.

Leon also helped several young men around that area to learn trades. He was a firm believer in learning as much as you could about everything, but he was especially keen on the idea of acquiring job skills, just in case things went bad in the music business. Just as he had been taught to lay brick by his cousin Bartley Walls, Leon taught some of his sons, as well as their cousins and friends, the skills of being a brick mason. If a child expressed an interest in working and earning some extra spending money, Pop would find a way to put him to work. His first son Bill eventually became a brick contractor himself, and Huey, Frank, Leonard, Melvin, and Doug would all know the feel of brick. Plenty of sweat from the Williams boys had been added to the mortar as they mixed it by hand on the hot summer days during a brick-laying job contracted by their father. When Leonard and Melvin later attended community college, both took some trade courses, Leonard in refrigeration and air-conditioning and Melvin in welding.

Leon also made time for his church. Unlike many people who forget their roots when they acquire a bit of fame, Pop Williams and his family never did. His groups sang at Rose Hill Missionary Baptist Church and other local churches whenever they could. Pop himself served on the Cemetery Committee and helped raised money to buy a new steeple for the church. He was always available to help organize a fundraiser performance for this project or that one around the church or the community.

Though Pop endured the unfortunate racism that touched the lives of all African Americans, he never became bitter. In fact, if a white person was in need, Leon would offer help readily. When hurricane Camille devastated the area in 1969, Pop Williams organized a performance at Rose Hill to raise money for the many people whose homes had been damaged. When it came time to distribute the money to those in need, he insisted that white families as well as black families receive some of the funds.

But Leon wasn't the only one who helped those in need. In her quiet way, Amanda provided a support system in her family, her church, and her community that made it possible for others to experience success. Never one to seek attention for herself, she usually pursued activities that were more in the background. For example, during the 1970s when her children no longer needed as much attention, Amanda went to work at a discount department store in McComb, F&C Dollar Store.

At other times in her life, she involved herself in volunteer work, such as providing in-home care for the elderly or the sick. Amanda was such a dependable care-giver that people soon started asking her if she knew others who might be able to provide the same kind of services. Amanda spread the word at her church and with her neighbors. In the months to come after that, she could be seen driving throughout the Smithdale area in her station wagon, picking up as many as eleven women. She would take them to their respective jobs in McComb, then pick them up at the end of the day and bring them home.

The Williams family became known and respected in Smithdale, McComb, and even beyond. In the years to come, when the children gained national fame, people began watching the family closely. Would all the attention affect them like it had many others, causing them to ignore those they had grown up with? Pop made sure that never happened. "Everyone is someone," he would tell them. "Never think you are better than anyone else. One day you might be up and the next day you might be down, then you would need a helping hand. Make sure you offer that helping hand to others when you see they need you."

Melvin would one day record a song by the name of "The Old Man" that was clearly inspired by the example his father set for him. The song was mainly a "talking" tune in which Melvin gave a narration while playing his acoustic guitar:

"This is a story about an old man who could barely read or write—and one day when he went to his mailbox, he noticed some young boys on the sidewalk, laughing and making fun of him because he was struggling and straining to read his mail.

"And one morning the man stopped and said, 'Young men, I wanna know what's so funny?'

"He said, 'Instead of laughin' at me you oughta be thankful you can go to school and get a good education.'

"He said, 'I didn't have a chance to go to school like you. I had to work in the fields, pickin' cotton and plowin' the old mules from sun-up to sundown, just to provide food and clothes for my family. But by the help of the good Lord, we made it.'

"The old man said, 'I may not have book sense like you, but I've been saved and got the love of Jesus in my heart, and He's my teacher. He taught me how to love one another, how to give and be forgiving.'

"He said, 'Young men, you may grow up to be lawyers and teachers, but if you don't have the love of Jesus in your hearts, it don't mean a thing.'"

The chorus of Melvin's song summed it up.

> *He said, "I can't read like you."*
> *He said, "I can't write like you do.*
> *But my name has been written down*
> *In the Lamb's book of life.*
> *And when the book of life is opened*
> *And the roll call is read,*
> *Jesus will be there . . . to read my name." ***

---

* | *By Melvin Williams. © 1999, Melvin Williams Music.*

CHAPTER V

nd Now. . .
The Williams Brothers

*Doug smiles as he thinks back
over the years. From the
time he was in grade school,
he has waited in many
places for the group to
be introduced. For
three decades,
he and
Melvin
and the
family friend Henry have brought their music to crowds both large and small, at churches
and concert halls and auditoriums across the country and in Europe. They are The
Williams Brothers, the gospel singing group that people have grown to love.*

So, he asks himself, why are there butterflies in my stomach tonight?

*He smiles at Terrell Gatlin, the backup singer and bass guitar player who has been
with The Williams Brothers since 1979, and at the other members of the band crowded
together: drummer Quincy McCullum, guitarist Ron Artis, keyboardist Nathan Barnes,
and organist Norman Williams. The group has made a lot of music over the years, and the
Lord has used their talents to minister to literally millions through their performances and
recordings. Now, here they are, standing in a tiny hallway. It reminds him of the early
days of The Williams Brothers.*

The Williams household was always a place of music, so all the children were involved in music and singing during their younger years. ("They could sneeze and it would sound good," boyhood friend and cousin Theodis Westbrook used to say.) Over the years, they would choose different directions for their lives. Not all would choose to stay close to home, but eventually even those who moved far away would return to the state of their birth.

Bill would become an independent brick contractor, like his father. Deliana would marry, move to Detroit with her husband Willie Banks (also a gospel singer), then to Jackson, Mississippi, and eventually back to Smithdale, right down the road from what all the children knew as The Big House, the home in which she had grown up. Huey and Frank would both become members of The Jackson Southernaires, and Frank would also go to work for Malaco Records in Jackson, the state capital. Josie Marie would move to California to work in the electronics industry but in the late 1970s she would return to live in Smithdale. In 1988 Leonard would leave The Williams Brothers to form his own company, Melendo Records, in Jackson. The three youngest Williams children—Melvin, Marilyn, and Doug, along with Henry—would found their own record company, and though their company would be closer to Smithdale than Leonard's, the results of their efforts would be known the world over.

In the late 1950s, however, all those choices were decades away. On Sunday afternoons the second batch of Williams kids would play church in the yard, mimicking the way they had so often seen their older brothers and sisters perform. Leonard, Melvin, Marilyn, and even little toddler Doug, all swaying and singing, crooned into broomstick microphones, absolutely positive that they sounded just as polished as their older siblings had when they sang with The Southern Gospel Singers.

"I remember we had made up this little song with nonsense words— 'Hobbee Deebee Dobbee Di'—and we used to go out in the yard singing that over and over to different tunes. But then we started learning other songs with real words and we sang those out there in the yard too, acting like we were our older brothers and sisters performing in front of people," says Melvin.

On one of those Sunday afternoons, Pop Williams once again paused in his conversation with friends inside the house to listen to his children singing. Once again he noticed how good they sounded. And once again he decided to give them the chance to make music for the Lord.

Some cousins—Edward Cain was one—were added to the mix, and a new group of young male singers was launched—The Little Williams Brothers. (Marilyn didn't perform with the group, but she was always close by and eventually became the group's office manager.) Leonard and Melvin were leaders of the group; on occasion they were joined by older brother Frank.

Doug remembers those early days.

"In a family like ours, that always had music, we took it for granted. We were singing as soon as we could walk. Everyone was singing; it was all around us, a family tradition. Even before I started elementary, when I stayed with my grandmother while everyone was out working or traveling with the group, I was at home playing those big 78 records all day. I would learn those songs word for word, from groups like The Five Blind Boys of Mississippi, The Five Blind Boys of Alabama, The Mighty Clouds of Joy, The Sensational Nightingales, The Davis Sisters, The Caravans. I remember songs like 'Christian Automobile' by the Dixie Hummingbirds and 'Bedside of a Neighbor.' I would sing along with them on the lead and later would pick up singing in harmony from singing with my brothers.

"Even though I was shy as a boy, I knew that I wanted to sing; it was just in me. I would be in the living room, acting like I was up before people, backing up those records and playing them over and over again."

Little Doug's musical talent was already clearly in evidence. The day came when Pop decided to let the five-year-old come along with the group and sing lead on one song.

"I got up and sang 'O Lord, I'm Your Child,' a hit song by The Hightower Brothers, and then after I sat down on the pew, I burst out crying. I was overcome with emotion from what I had just done, I guess," Doug said.

As had been his practice when he started The Southern Gospel Singers, Pop worked hard all week on the farm or doing his "public work" of bricklaying or carpentry. After work, he oversaw the new group of youngsters as they met for their practice sessions at night. On the weekends, he loaded the group of singers into his old car and took them to perform for churches in the area. Pop knew that many of the churches would never be able to afford to pay the young singing group, but that didn't stop him. He was perfectly willing to finance their travels. He didn't question that this was a good use of his money, and even during the winters when construction was slow, he would find a way to take the boys to their engagements.

Of course, at times that meant hiding the car to keep an ambitious bill collector from repossessing it. Pop and the boys would roll the car behind some bushes and, then, when the repo man came snooping around, they would turn out all the lights and pretend no one was home. But Pop always caught up on the payments when the work came in. And he always used the family car for the Lord's work, just as his mother Eula had insisted on doing, using it for her missionary trips when he was a boy.

Word of mouth spread the group's reputation, and invitations came in from churches across the southern parts of Mississippi, Louisiana, and Alabama. The boys settled into a routine, dividing their time among school work, farm work, practicing their music, and performing on the weekends. In the summers, they worked with their dad laying brick, and they also increased the number of performances they gave, singing at revivals and camp meetings. The schedule was demanding, but they had never known it to be any other way.

"We would practice at the house a lot of times," Doug remembers. "We didn't have a piano at that time, so we would just use guitars, right there in the living room. There would be a bunch of people there sometimes, and we would practice until 11 or 12 at night. Pop would sit and listen and give us instructions. We didn't have any air conditioning so, especially in the summertime, we would be wringing wet with sweat."

Pop felt good about the group's sound, but he recognized that there was a musical hole to be filled, and none of the family members had exactly what he was looking for. He wanted a strong voice that was able to sing a high tenor harmony when necessary.

It was in 1961 that one of the Williams cousins told Pop about another singer, Henry Green, he had heard sing at the Brown's Chapel Primitive Baptist Church in Liberty, only a few miles from Smithdale. The third of 12 children, Henry had worked the fields until he was old enough to go to work, first in a Phillips 66 service station, and then at Eisworth Motors, a Ford dealership, both in McComb. In 1961 Henry was 18 years old, a year older than Josie Marie Williams, and like the Williams children, Henry had grown up with music.

"A lot of people don't realize what it was like back then," remembers Henry. "We sang because we loved singing, and whatever we had to do to support ourselves, we would do. He also recalls that when he was very young, he and a friend, Sonny Jackson, would walk for miles along the rural Mississippi roads, two boys looking for others, any others, to sing with. They would sing on front porches, they would sing as they walked along, they would sing out in the yard. Often they gathered under a big oak tree to sing "When the Saints Go Marchin' In."

One day Reverend L. C. McCray heard the boys singing there, and was so moved that he preached under the old oak's outstretched branches while a new church building, the Holy Hill Church, was raised on that spot. (The original church has since been torn down, but there is still a church on the same site.)

When Pop Williams went to hear Henry at Brown's Chapel Church, he liked how the young man could hit the high notes (years later gospel great Vicki Winans nicknamed Henry "Squeaky" because of his talent for hitting those notes) yet still blend in with the other singers. "Cousin Henry"—or "Mr. Green," as he is still sometimes called—became the newest member of The Little Williams Brothers.

With that last piece of the puzzle in place, Pop made sure the group performed as often as possible. Maybe because he was older than the others, Henry was close to Pop and would even share a hotel room with him when on the road. A quiet person with a ready smile, Henry was in many ways Pop's opposite. Melvin and Doug remember that Pop seemed to open up to Henry on those long road trips, perhaps because Henry said little but when he spoke, his words were usually wise ones.

The popularity of The Little Williams Brothers grew throughout the 1960s. In 1965 they became The Sensational Williams Brothers, but it wasn't until 1979 that they became just The Williams Brothers.* During school months, they performed nearly every weekend at churches throughout the South. During the summer, when the boys were out of school, Pop would sometimes arrange for appearances at showcases, and even organized brief tours.

One summer tour that all remember was a 1966 trip to California. Josie Marie had recently moved to Silicon Valley, and had booked the group into several churches in the area. The challenge was getting there.

Pop Williams was still working his job as a brick contractor, keeping up the farm, and managing the group on the side. When they traveled anywhere, he footed the bill. That included loading up the seven or so group members in his car and heading out for whatever destination they had booked. The heat of this summer trip was too much for his old car, however, which pooped out in Big

* | *Although the pre-1979 group was officially The Sensational Williams Brothers, both lineups are hereafter referred to simply as The Williams Brothers.*

Spring, Texas, midway between Abilene and the New Mexico border. He knew no one in the area, but Pop didn't seem to worry about details like that. He called a few churches and made arrangements for his young men to stay the night at church members' homes. In exchange, The Williams Brothers arranged a couple of performances for the group, raised enough money to repair the car, and they were on their way again to California for more bookings, all of which were good experiences for the young group.

Henry Green woke up one Monday morning in the late 1960s feeling uneasy. He hadn't told anyone yet, but he had decided to get out of the music business.

As he went about preparing to leave for work at his mechanic's job, Henry thought about all the negative comments he had heard from family and friends during the past few years.

"Give up this crazy dream," they said. "Get a real job where you can take care of your family. You'll never become a professional gospel singer."

He had heard it so often, he had finally started believing it.

Henry gathered up his bagged lunch and headed out the door, lost in thought. This was the right thing to do. After all, he had a good job with Carruth Construction. What was he doing traveling all over the country on weekends singing with the Williams family? Sometimes he got home so late on Sunday night that he barely had time to change his clothes before it was time to leave for work on Monday morning.

He had been thinking about quitting for a while. He had just bought a new house in Summit and needed to keep his steady work so he could make his house note each month.

Henry knew he had let everyone down this past weekend by not showing up to leave for the concert at the little church in north Mississippi. But he just couldn't go; he couldn't do it anymore.

He got up and went to work Monday morning as usual. He hadn't been there long, however, when he saw Pop's pickup truck coming down the road. Henry's heart sank. He hadn't expected to have to face the consequences of his decision so soon. Pop waved the younger man over and the two sat on the tailgate of the pickup.

"What is the problem, son?" Pop asked.

"I'm just not a singer," Henry said.

Pop looked steadily at the other man for a moment. "Henry, you are anything you want to be in life, once you've set your heart and mind to it. As far as Leonard, Melvin, Doug, and I are concerned, you are a singer. If you weren't, I wouldn't have asked you to join the group when I first heard you sing 'I Know I've Been Changed.'"

Henry dropped his head. "I just don't know. I need to make sure that I can pay my house note and light bill each month. I'm not sure I can do that just by singing."

Pop didn't answer for a moment. "Make me a promise."

Henry looked up. "Promise what?"

"Promise me that you will stick with the group. I know it is going to work. And I will promise you that your bills will be paid each month."

Henry stared at the older man. If he knew one thing about Pop, it was that he didn't make promises lightly and he always kept his word. Pop's faith in what they were doing was good enough for Henry.

"I promise," he said.

In the years to come, Pop kept his promise to Henry, though sometimes it wasn't easy to do.

During their early years of traveling, the group performed in some odd places and under some less than ideal conditions. But that made for entertaining war stories in the years to come, stories that capture the ups and downs experienced by most groups on the road.

Like the time Pop scheduled The Williams Brothers to sing for an event in Jackson, an anniversary performance honoring another gospel group, The Bright Stars. After the concert, the group split up to stay at the homes of people they knew in the area. Pop and Melvin, who was still just a boy at the time, spent the night at the home of Murray C. Johnson, one of the concert organizers and the manager of The Bright Stars, who Pop knew was also an organizer in the civil rights movement.

At about 4 a.m., a deafening BOOM sounded. An explosion rocked the house, blowing out walls and collapsing some of the roof and ceilings. Pop and Melvin, who were sharing a bed, awoke with a jolt. A 2 by 6 board dislodged from the ceiling had fallen, and would have hit them if it hadn't been deflected by the headboard.

Everyone stumbled out of the house and into the street as the sirens wailed in the distance. At first everyone suspected a bomb, but later it was found that the explosion had been caused by a faulty gas heater.

On a lighter note, Melvin had more pressing concerns than what had caused the house he was sleeping in to explode around him. As he stood in the cold in his underwear, he looked at the house and then looked up at his dad before he delivered a line that was to be repeated often in the years that followed.

"Dad, *now* where we gonna eat at?"

Then there was the time they drove to Alabama one Saturday to sing for a church service the next day. Despite a blinding rainstorm, they were able to reach the home of the pastor that afternoon, and, following a home-cooked meal, they retired for the night. Next morning, they started on their way to the church. To say the church was off the beaten path was an understatement. The pastor had written directions for the group because he and his wife had to be at the church early and had left before the Williams boys and Pop finished breakfast. The directions didn't help Pop deal with the quagmire that the dirt road had become after the previous day's deluge. Pop gingerly prodded the car down the road like an old mule, trying to keep from getting stuck as the mud sucked at the tires. Soon the church was in sight. There was just one small problem.

Between the car and the church was a rain-swollen creek with only one way across: a narrow, rickety, weather-beaten wood bridge. Pop stopped the car and peered at the bridge, scratching his head. Some of the slats of the bridge had rotted through and others had already fallen away so that, at certain places, you could see the water rushing below. As they looked at it, they could hear the old wood of the bridge creaking and moaning. Henry could have sworn he saw the whole thing swaying.

Pop nodded to himself. He had decided they would cross it.

"You boys walk across, one by one," he said, "and then you can guide me across in the car from the other side."

As much as the boys loved Pop and trusted his driving ability, they didn't complain about having to walk across. Before they trudged through the mud to the bridge, they rolled their pants legs up to their knees. There was nothing worse than trying to get dried red clay mud off your clothes. Then they started across the creek.

Once safe on the other side, they turned and signaled Pop. He inched the car forward, not daring to move more than a foot or two at a time. The boys could hear the wood of the old bridge straining as it bent under the weight of the car. Each of them held his breath and let a silent prayer go up to the Lord. "Let it hold together, at least until Pop gets across."

Pop was holding his breath as well. He leaned his head out of the window, making sure he was keeping the tires straight on the narrow bridge. Nobody breathed until Pop rolled those last few inches onto solid ground again.

Before continuing to the church, Pop made sure they cleaned the red clay off their shoes because he always wanted his singers to make a good appearance. Cleaned up and ready to perform, they arrived at the church and walked into the sanctuary.

There sat the only two people who had come to the concert: Reverend Smitty and his wife.

The perils of nature The Williams Brothers faced as they pursued their calling were not confined to bad weather.

Once Pop had booked the group into a small church in Monticello, Mississippi, just forty or so miles from their home. When they arrived, they found that there was no separate room for them to change their clothes in the tiny church. So Doug, Melvin, Henry, Leonard, friend Thomas Barnes, and Charles Gayden, a cousin playing with the group at the time, took their uniforms and started for a wood thicket just behind the church.

Pop held their clothes for them while they changed. Unfortunately, their stomping through the woods had disturbed the thicket's inhabitants. The damp brush and hot, humid Mississippi air made for an ideal breeding ground for some of the biggest mosquitoes the boys had ever seen. As they took off their shirts, the giant mosquitoes attacked. Before long the boys' backs and arms and necks were covered with the insects. Pop swiped at their backs with the arm-load of clothes he was holding. The boys kept moving, in a frenzied dance, on the theory that it was harder to hit a moving target. After what seemed to them an eternity, they got their uniforms on and galloped for the church, bursting through the doors laughing and in disarray. But they sang just the same.

Then there was the time, in another one-room church, this one in Utica, a little town just outside Jackson, Mississippi, that some nonwinged animals got more attention than the group did.

The church was made of cinderblock, providing ready-made hidey-holes for anything small and flexible enough to slither inside. About midway through the performance, Henry glanced over at the side wall and noticed that the audience had grown by three. Some six-inch-long green lizards had decided they enjoyed the music and had emerged from the crevices in the walls to get a better view. But these new gospel fans were not satisfied to sit quietly. They were crawling along the wall, heading for a front row seat.

Unfortunately for everyone involved, the pastor of the church caught a glimpse of the lizards at the same time. He grabbed a broom and headed for the green intruders just as The Williams Brothers began singing.

"Wham!" The broom hit the wall and the lizards scattered. The group kept on singing.

"Wham!" The preacher swung the broom again, but the lizards were quicker than he was. One of the lizards made it to the front of the church and started across the floor and around the boys, who had never stopped singing. By now, the preacher was determined to get those lizards out of his church, and he darted after the sole escapee, brushing between Melvin and Doug to take another swipe with the broom.

The Williams Brothers kept on singing, though it was admittedly difficult to sing and laugh at the same time. The two other lizards saw their chance for freedom and dashed for the front door with the preacher in hot pursuit. By now the audience was gasping for breath between gales of laughter. (Later, the group would record a hit song that Doug insists was partially inspired by the sight of the pastor going after those lizards, "Sweep Around Your Own Front Door.")

The lizards weren't the only reptiles to attend a Williams Brothers concert. Years later, on a hot summer night in a Rocky Mount, North Carolina school gym with no air-conditioning, someone had left a side door near the stage open for ventilation. The Williams Brothers had just started to sing "Jesus Will Fix It" when they noticed the audience was responding in a most unusual way, running around, hollering, and screaming. The group was excited at first to see what they thought were expressions of enthusiasm, then noticed that a five-foot-long blacksnake had crawled into the gym and staked out a place in front of the stage to enjoy the music. After the school janitor had driven away the unwelcome fan, the concert continued, to a more usual audience reaction.

Pop and The Williams Brothers were to learn that another type of creature, the human animal, could be more threatening in some ways than the four-legged types.

In the early years especially, concerts in smaller churches might mean the group would be paid $150 to $200. Much later, bigger concerts might net $5,000 to $7,500 on a good night. The money was split five ways.

As Pop was a man of his word, Henry was always the first to be paid. And during the early days, the boys also decided that on the weekends when Henry's light bill or his house payment of $74.50 was due, he would get all the money that week.

The people that The Williams Brothers dealt with didn't always have a similar sense of fair play.

Once in the early '70s, Pop and the boys were in Illinois, having been booked by a promoter for two performances in one day. The first was to be early in the afternoon in Chicago and the second that evening in Joliet. In Chicago, after what Pop considered to be a good performance, he went back to the promoter's office to get their money.

"There's not going to be any money," the promoter told him. "I'm losing money on both concerts."

Pop let it slide for the time being, knowing that when the gate was small, the bigger-name groups might get all the profits from a concert. He had an uneasy feeling about the promoter, however, and made up his mind on the half-hour drive down to Joliet that he would ask the man again after the second performance. His boys had come a long way and it would be tough to explain how they were coming away from two performances with empty pockets.

On the stage in Joliet, the boys gave another great performance. (They could always tell they were doing well when they looked out at the audience and saw Pop in the front row, swaying and clapping with the rest of the crowd. If they could reach Pop, they knew they were reaching everyone.)

While the boys changed clothes and loaded the car for the long drive back to Mississippi, Pop slipped back to the promoter's office. There he sat, behind a table covered with stacks of tens, twenties, and fifties. One of his assistants was counting a stack of twenties. When Pop came in, the man stopped counting.

"My boys put on two great concerts for you," Pop said as he unbuttoned his jacket. In his belt was stuck the 38-caliber handgun he always carried in the car for protection. He pulled out the gun and laid it on the table atop the stacks of money.

Pop never raised his voice. In fact, he acted as if the gun weren't even there. He just kept looking at the promoter.

"They deserve to be paid," he said.

The promoter took one look at Pop's face and motioned to his assistant. The man hastily counted out the amount the contracts said The Williams Brothers would be paid and handed it to Pop.

Smiling, Pop stuck the gun back in his belt, and just before walking out the door he turned back to the promoter and said, "Thank you, gentlemen."

Not all of the group's troubles were due to dishonest promoters. As bad as that promoter had been, it wouldn't be long before the group itself would be the reason there was no money to share.

In 1970, the group was singing at a little community church just north of McComb. When they opened their mouths to sing "Jesus Will Fix It," they started off-key. The more they tried to correct the problem and find the right key, the worse they sounded. It didn't get better, and they were off on nearly every song they sang that night.

They didn't need the audience to tell them they were delivering an awful performance that evening. Pop sat stone-faced on the first pew all night. He didn't say a word to them until they pulled up in the front yard of the house in Smithdale.

"I'm not taking you boys out with y'all singing like that," he said.

At first, Melvin, Doug, Leonard, and Henry thought he was joking.

"I won't let you embarrass yourselves," he said. "Go rehearse and I'll let you know when we're going back on the road."

He got out of the car and went into the house. The others sat there for a moment, not sure what to say because they knew now that Pop was completely serious. Finally, Henry broke the silence. "I'll meet you here after work tomorrow to start rehearsing."

For the next few weeks they rehearsed daily from the time Henry got off work until late into the night. Several times, when they thought they were ready, they'd call Pop into the living room and sing for him. He'd listen, then just sit there and shake his head. "Not yet."

After two months, Pop again took a seat on his living room couch. As they sang, the four young men searched his face for some sign that he liked what he heard.

After the last tones of the song died away, Pop stood up. And smiled.

"Now I'll take you back out," he said.

The boys felt vindicated. They had pleased Pop.

CHAPTER VI

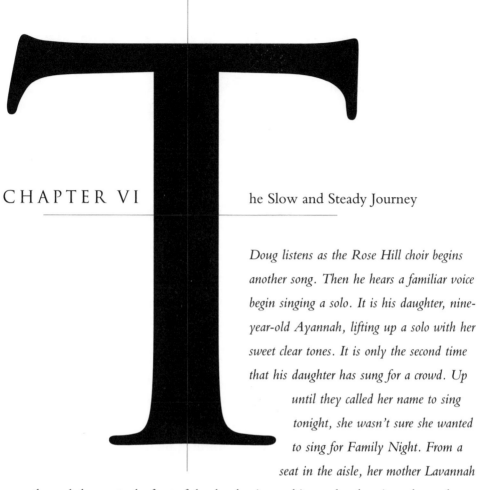

he Slow and Steady Journey

Doug listens as the Rose Hill choir begins another song. Then he hears a familiar voice begin singing a solo. It is his daughter, nine-year-old Ayannah, lifting up a solo with her sweet clear tones. It is only the second time that his daughter has sung for a crowd. Up until they called her name to sing tonight, she wasn't sure she wanted to sing for Family Night. From a seat in the aisle, her mother Lavannah gently sends her up to the front of the church. Ayannah's grandmother Amanda watches with pride as another generation of Williams family gospel music is offered to the Lord.

Out of the corner of her eye Mom Williams sees a movement. It is Doug, peeking out from the hallway where he is waiting, wanting to catch a glimpse of his daughter as she sings.

Amanda chuckles to herself. She remembers little Doug at the microphone as a boy, joining his big brothers in the group.

Doug smiled at himself in the mirror as he prepared to leave for school this morning. He was enjoying school and had even toyed with the idea of running track for the high school team. He was tall and athletic, and his legs were able to carry him a good deal faster than when those wasps had gone after him a dozen years ago.

He was looking forward to graduating from high school so that he could join Henry, his brothers, and the rest of the group on the road full-time.

It was 1973. The group had just released its first album, *Holding On,* on the Songbird label. People were starting to talk about this energetic group from Mississippi and the invitations to perform were coming from bigger auditoriums and events.

Not that the attention was going to the boys' heads. Pop still made sure of that. No one who met The Williams Brothers failed to notice their gentle spirits. Melvin, Leonard, Doug, Henry, and drummer Maurice Surrell didn't seem to have the kind of egos that so many rising musicians exhibited. They just wanted to make music for the Lord, music that people enjoyed, music that could lead them in worship and praise.

Doug walked back to the room he shared with his brother Melvin, who was three years older. Melvin was sitting on the side of the bed, still trying to shake the sleep from his head. He was performing music full-time now so he didn't have to worry about getting to school on time. Good thing, thought Doug as he gave his older—but shorter—brother a playful thump on his head in passing.

Leonard, Melvin, and Doug had been exposed to a number of different musical styles while growing up. At church, they learned the traditional hymns and choir-singing styles. In the group, they learned about quartet singing and how to blend their voices while performing as The Williams Brothers. And at school—Lillie Mae Bryant Elementary in Bude, Mississippi, and Liberty High School in Amite County—they broadened their musical horizons still more. Melvin, who also attended Southwest Junior College, attributes their amazing range as songwriters to this variety of musical influences in their lives.

"A lot of people don't realize that we had a lot of voice training," Melvin says, "especially in the school system with the choir directors there. We sang all kinds of stuff: classical, little jazz numbers, old Negro spirituals, patriotic songs. I remember Mr. Thomas at Liberty High School. He made us do it right."

By the early seventies, both Melvin and Doug had started writing songs for the group.

"Most of the times I will get the whole basic structure of a song in my head and I will show the bass line to some musicians, even before I get all the lyrics figured out. Because I know that if you get that bass line down, you can build on that. I create the song, then work with others to build on it. We will get the hook and a title, then a chorus and maybe a bridge. Then I might go back and forth until the words start flowing," says Doug.

The two had learned to make beautiful gospel music on stage, but their personalities were different as could be. Melvin had earned the nickname "Bunny Rabbit" from his older sister Ree because he liked to hop from one thing to another. He was full of curiosity about things, particularly anything musical, and he had a versatility that allowed him to switch gears faster than most people. When he was quite young, he taught himself to play on Frank's guitar. But Melvin was left-handed, so in order to play the chords, he would have had to restring the guitar so that the bottom string was at the top, and so forth. That option wasn't open to him, so he just turned Frank's guitar upside down and figured out how to play his chords upside down and backwards. (He still plays left-handed today on his upside-down guitar, tuning it to an open E chord). His proficiency allowed him to learn enough on several instruments to fill in for the band's musicians if needed, even though his place was more and more in the front singing and leading the group.

It was in the studio that Melvin shined because he was able to jump from one part of a song to another and immediately get a feel for how the parts fit together musically to give the extra touch a tune needed. Studio musicians might smile at Melvin's exuberance, but they were sometimes slightly miffed at his insistence that the music be "just right." But that's how Pop had taught him to be: Never settle for less than the best from yourself.

Doug possessed a singing voice that matched Melvin's or anyone else in the family, but he was a bit more methodical than his closest older brother. He was able to see the big picture clearly and always seemed to be thinking about where The Williams Brothers group was heading in its ministry. Some said he took after his brother Frank, able to mix his creative talents with an ability to manage people well. While Melvin was flitting from one thing to another, always making things better one bit at a time, Doug was steadily focusing on the main direction for the group. What road should they take? What lay ahead for them?

By the early 1970s, Pop began to feel that The Williams Brothers group was ready for some professional recording experience.

By 1971, older brothers Huey and Frank were living in Jackson and singing with the gospel group The Jackson Southernaires on the Songbird Record label. Previously, Huey had lived with his sister Deliana and her husband Willie Banks in Detroit for years. While in Detroit, Huey had first worked at a carwash, then at a butcher shop for nearly a decade while singing with a group called Henry Harris and the Flying Clouds. In 1960 he left Detroit for New Orleans, where he worked as a bricklayer for three years.

In the meantime, Willie Banks and Deliana had moved to Jackson, where Willie joined The Jackson Southernaires. Huey came back to Jackson for what he thought was a temporary stay before moving to California. He found a few bricklaying jobs to raise money for the trip west, and stayed with his sister's family. While there, a vacancy opened up with The Jackson Southernaires and the group approached Huey for a tryout. He was accepted and decided to sing with the group a while. A few months passed, then a year, and the temporary stay turned into a permanent relationship with The Jackson Southernaires. During that time Huey also met his wife-to-be Mamie Gibson, a singer with the gospel group The Gloriettes. When Frank came to Jackson to attend college, he also joined The Jackson Southernaires, which gained recognition with their 1967 gospel hit, "Too Late," on the Songbird/Peacock label.

In 1970, Huey approached Don Robey, an executive at Peacock Records, and asked him to consider releasing an album by The Williams Brothers. Robey balked at the idea, not sure he wanted to take a chance on a local group with unproven appeal on the national level. Besides, their style was a little more contemporary than that of The Jackson Southernaires; he wasn't sure that Peacock's buying audience would go for the songs of this young Williams Brothers group.

"I tell you what," Robey told Huey, "if you think they are so good, then let them have the other side of the next Southernaires album."

Huey consulted with the rest of The Jackson Southernaires and they agreed to try a joint project with The Williams Brothers. That combination album, *He's My Brother,* with the Jackson Southernaires—with brothers Huey and Frank—on one side, and The Williams Brothers—featuring brothers Melvin, Leonard, and Doug, and Henry Green—on the other side, was released in 1971. The blend of musical styles apparently appealed to many gospel music fans, for the album sold well.

Pop Williams started making bigger plans then, and pushed for The Williams Brothers' first stand-alone album on Songbird Records. Songbird agreed to release the album in 1973.

All the Williams sons had been writing songs for years, so they felt confident they could put together their own album. They started sorting through the possibilities and in early 1973 were able to release their first album, *Holding On,* which included the song "Jesus Will Fix It," an old song that The Williams Brothers had reworked a bit by adding their own unique sound to it.

"I remember that we finished recording the album at Songbird's studio in Houston, Texas," says Doug, "and Don Robey took us across the street and bought us dinner, hamburgers and fries. That was our pay for the album." That wasn't unusual for a new gospel group during those times and, besides, it was worth it just to have an album on the top gospel record label in the nation at that time.

Not one member of the group was prepared for the attention this album would garner. "Jesus Will Fix It" became an instant hit and got so much play on the radio that *Holding On* rose to number one on the Billboard national gospel charts within three months after its release.

Suddenly, the whole world looked different for The Williams Brothers. They had turned a corner.

As the album started selling across the nation, they began getting invitations for bookings from people they had never heard of. Moreover, promoters who had even just recently turned them down for showcases because of their lack of name recognition were now calling them, trying to book the group for their concerts.

"I remember we got a call from a promoter who was putting together a concert at the City Auditorium in Atlanta, featuring Reverend James Cleveland and Shirley Caesar," says Doug. "It was the biggest thing we had been part of at that time; we didn't even know how much to tell them we got for a performance. We called Frank and he said, 'Try $500.' And we did. That was the most money we had received for a performance up till then."

In the spring of 1974, after the release of *Holding On,* Doug graduated from high school and was able to travel with the group full-time.

Invitations for singing engagements continued to come in during the rest of 1973, and in 1974, Songbird released the second Williams Brothers album, *What's Wrong With the People Today?* That year, the group went on its first national tour with The Jackson Southernaires, traveling to the West Coast again. This time, however, they would have bookings laid out for the tour ahead of time, instead of playing it day to day as they had done on their cross-country trip in Pop's car in the mid-sixties.

Gospel radio stations throughout America were giving more play to Williams Brothers songs, and as their name recognition grew, they were booked to do more concerts. In 1976, *Spreading a Message* was released on the Nashboro label and, on the popularity of the hit song "Jesus Will Never Say No," rose to number one on the *Billboard* gospel chart. That album's success resulted in The Williams Brothers being invited to join another national tour that year, this time with Willie Neal Johnson and The Gospel Keynotes, The Fantastic Violinaires, and The Five Blind Boys of Mississippi. That tour covered more cities than the previous one, taking the group up the East Coast from Florida to New York—including several performances at the famous Apollo Theater in New York City's Harlem—then out west again to California.

Pop Williams's work ethic kept the group plugging away, both at performing and songwriting. In 1977, two Williams Brothers albums were released by Savoy Records: *Mama Prayed for Me* and *Taking Gospel Higher,* which rose to number four on the *Billboard* gospel chart on the strength of the single "I Won't Let Go of My Faith."

The first two Williams Brothers national tours were basically in front of traditional gospel audiences, that is, audiences that came to hear music in the tradition of the black gospel choir and the quartet. Their third national tour, in 1977, would give The Williams Brothers a little broader exposure. This tour, with Walter Hawkins and The Hawkins Family from Oakland, California, would also reach audiences for "contemporary gospel," a term describing gospel music with a strong rhythm and blues, or soul, component. The tour included performances at some of the larger venues for gospel music: the Paramount Theatre in Oakland; the Fox Theatre in St. Louis, and Brooklyn Academy in New York.

The tour with the Hawkins Family also proved, however, that just because they had started receiving national attention, they were not exempt from negative experiences on the road. One promoter in New York at a sold-out house flatly told The Williams Brothers that he didn't respect their music and that they could go on stage and perform but he wasn't going to pay them. The group refused to go on. When the Hawkins Family asked about the delay, they were told about the promoter's refusal to pay. The Hawkins Family immediately told the promoter that they would not perform either unless he kept his agreement to pay The Williams Brothers. The promoter relented.

The Lord kept blessing the group. More albums were forthcoming, including *I've Got a Home* and *Celebrate This Christmas* on Savoy Records in 1978, and *First Class Gospel* on Tomato Records in 1979. Also in 1979, another tour invitation came along that would take The Williams Brothers to yet another level.

The call came in from Reverend James Cleveland, who personally asked The Williams Brothers to join his next national gospel tour, "The World's Greatest Gospel Show."* In addition to Reverend Cleveland, the tour would include a veritable "Who's Who" in the world of black gospel, including Shirley Caesar, The Gospel Keynotes, Inez Andrews, and The Mighty Clouds of Joy.

This tour allowed The Williams Brothers to appear in front of their largest crowds ever, including performances at Cobo Arena in Detroit (13,000 people), Cook Convention Center in Memphis (12,000), The Summit in Houston (8,000), and the Coliseum in Charlotte, North Carolina (10,000). The tour lasted a year and propelled the group into a spiral of growth—and even more hard work.

---

* | *Reverend James Cleveland, who passed away in 1991, is one of the most respected names in the world of gospel. Founder of the Gospel Music Workshop of America, which is dedicated to preserving and nurturing gospel as an African-American art form and cultural tradition, Rev. Cleveland influenced the music and careers of many of today's popular gospel singers, and was the first black gospel artist to receive a star on Hollywood's Walk of Fame.*

The entire country was finding out about The Williams Brothers, and they liked what they were learning.

The group kept pressing forward in the early 1980s, releasing the album *God Will See You Through* in 1980 on New Birth Records, and *Brother to Brother*—with the hit song "He'll Understand"—in 1982 on Word Records.

The Williams Brothers spent more and more time on the road, with many single performance engagements. The group's popularity had risen to the point that they felt they didn't need national tours to increase their exposure. Invitations were coming for concerts and anniversary performances from other groups and from choirs and churches. In 1979, in the tradition of Pop's adage "Have Your Own," they decided to start their own booking agency rather than rely on someone else to schedule their performances. They called their new company Blackberry Entertainment. Marilyn Williams quit her job as a schoolteacher to help run the booking agency, which started out in a small one-room building next to the Williams family home in Smithdale. The office was so small that there was barely enough room for the two-sided desk that Marilyn was later to share with Walter Tackett when he came to work for the young company in the mid-1980s.

In the early 1980s, both Melvin and Doug got married, Melvin in December of 1981 to Donnice Jenkins, from Jayess, Mississippi, and Doug in July of 1982 to Lavannah Beauchamp, from Baton Rouge, Louisiana. Actually, the story goes, Doug met Lavannah's Aunt Gwen Royal first, at a concert in Baton Rouge. "Do you have someone back at home who has pretty legs like you do?" Doug asked the aunt in a rare moment of assertiveness. She said she did as a matter of fact and eventually set up a blind date for him to meet her niece on his next trip to Baton Rouge. At their first dinner date, all the assertiveness seemed to have left him, Lavannah remembers. "He was so nervous, he didn't even eat anything," she laughs.

Neither marriage slowed the group's pace, and there was no time for honeymoons. "I remember that we decided one morning to get married, and we did," says Doug. "Then that same day, I went back to the recording studio in Bogalusa, Louisiana." Doug and Lavannah did, however, move to McComb to raise Fumiko, Lavannah's daughter and Doug's stepdaughter. Lavannah got a job teaching third grade at Eva Gordon Elementary School in Magnolia, a small town about five miles south of McComb, and in the fall of 1983 Ayannah was born.

In 1983, The Williams Brothers recorded *Feel the Spirit* with Word Records and were scheduled also to release their album *Blessed* with Word in 1985. With all the studio work already completely finished, one of the executives decided he didn't like one of the songs, "I'm Just a Nobody," and tried to make The Williams Brothers go back into the studio.

Though they were young men, the members of The Williams Brothers had years of music experience behind them at that point. They knew that the Word executive was making a bad decision. So they made a decision of their own.

They took the *Blessed* album to Malaco Records in Jackson. Malaco had made its name as a label for rhythm and blues artists, but with the help of Frank Williams they had opened a Gospel Division in the early 1980s. They welcomed The Williams Brothers project and released *Blessed* in 1985.

The song "I'm Just a Nobody" not only hit number one on the *Billboard* gospel chart, staying there for over three months, but became the biggest hit The Williams Brothers have had to date. In addition, the video for "I'm Just a Nobody" was the first video Malaco produced for any of its artists, either secular or gospel.

The Williams Brothers continued to write music, record, and perform with some of the most famous names in the nation. In 1986 they came out with another Malaco release, *Hand in Hand,* which included the hits "God Will Deliver," "The Goat," and "Sweep Around Your Own Front Door." (Walter Tackett, who served as road manager for the group at that time, remembers that when The Williams Brothers first sang "The Goat" at a concert in Albany, Georgia, people actually rushed up to the stage applauding and screaming their approval. "Now, this was a gospel concert, not a rock concert. It was electrifying that night.") In 1988 came *A New Beginning* on Melendo Records. (Melendo had been formed the same year by Leonard Williams; see page 109.) Also that year, Melvin released his first solo album, *Back to the Cross,* on Light Records. Then in 1989 came another Malaco release, *Ain't Love Wonderful,* with the hit song "A Ship Like Mine."

Many people have ideas about why the appeal of The Williams Brothers is so strong. "They are very lively on stage, but they come across as very real— because they are real," says Tackett. "And they are versatile. They are one of the few quartet-style groups who could sing with Luther Vandross one day, then sing with Kirk Franklin the next, then perform on the same bill with the Happy Goodman Family or Amy Grant the next."

Edward Cain, one of the Williams cousins who was an original member of the group, singing with them from the early through the late sixties (Cain is now a captain in the McComb Fire Department), thinks the ensemble skills of the three up-front singers are a big factor:

"Melvin can come out for a performance and he will watch the crowd real well and feel their mood. That way, he knows just what to offer the crowd at a certain time, changing to meet them wherever they are. He never loses a crowd, which is the mark of a true lead singer in a group.

"Now Doug, he is a more spiritual type singer and can take a good slow song, like a hymn, and really get the crowd going with it. They are a real good combination working together, and can pick up from each other the ebb and flow of a song as well as anyone I've seen.

"And Henry Green is one of the best tenors on the road today."

In the career ahead of them, The Williams Brothers were to record 18 albums that made it to the top ten list in *Billboard* and *Cashbox* magazines. Three number one records and three Grammy nominations came out of those albums, and a number of songs became favorites of their fans: "Jesus Will Never Say No," "I Won't Let Go of My Faith," "He'll Understand," "Sweep Around Your Own Front Door," "The Goat," "I'm Just a Nobody," "How I Depend On You," "Somebody Needs You Lord," "If I Don't Wake Up," "God Will Deliver," "Never Could Have Made It Without You," and "A Ship Like Mine," to name a few. The group was also to perform at many prestigious events, including Black Expo, Operation Push, Budweiser Jazz Festivals, Gospel Music Workshop of America, Dove Awards, Kentucky's Gospel Festival, McDonald's Gospel Festival, National Council of Negro Women, B.R.E. (Black Radio Enterprise) Convention, C.O.G.I.C. (Church of God in Christ) Convention, the New Orleans Jazz Festival, and the National Baptist Convention, where they performed live with Stevie Wonder on "I'm Too Close" and on several songs from his *Songs in the Key of Life* album.

Among the venues where the group would perform were Madison Square Garden, Cobo Hall, Radio City Music Hall, the Apollo Theater, Disneyland, Disney World, Brooklyn Academy of Music, The Grand Ole Opry, Carnegie Hall, Front Row Theater, Paramount Theater, and many colleges and universities across the United States.

They would perform with a wide variety of artists: Stevie Wonder, Deneice Williams, Mighty Clouds of Joy, Luther Vandross, Phillip Bailey, The Mississippi Mass Choir, Maurice White, Andraé Crouch, Shirley Caesar, James Cleveland, Al Green, Kool and The Gang, BeBe and CeCe Winans, Vanessa Bell Armstrong, Patti LaBelle, The Hawkins Family, The Clark Sisters, Clifton Davis, Shirley Murdock, Sounds of Blackness, Kirk Franklin, and Amy Grant.

And the awards would come also. They received several Stellar Awards for Best Group (Traditional) in 1986, Album of the Year in 1987, Best Performance Group or Duo (Traditional) in 1991 and 1995, and would even receive The Stellar Vision Award in 1992. They would be nominated for a Grammy in 1991 for *This Is Your Night,* and in 1995 for *In This Place.* In 1996, Doug would receive Stellar awards as Male Vocalist of the Year and Contemporary Male Vocalist of the Year, and a Grammy nomination. Melvin would also be nominated for a Grammy in 1989.

The Williams Brothers' music ministry kept growing through the eighties. With each success, Leonard, Melvin, Doug, and Henry gave thanks to God, never feeling quite worthy for receiving such attention just for doing what they loved so much. They made sure they didn't keep the glory all to themselves.

Right about the time The Williams Brothers were breaking onto the national gospel scene, Pop Williams saw fit to make some other contacts that would help his "boys," as he called them, long into the future. One of those contacts was Mike Frascogna. Frascogna, a young attorney in Jackson, Mississippi, was one of the few handling entertainers as clients at that time and word of him reached Leonard, who suggested that Pop look him up.

Frascogna was a solo practitioner with a practice barely a year old when Pop Williams showed up unannounced at his office in the Quarter on Lakeland Drive in Jackson in 1973.

"I want to find my boys a lawyer, one who knows the entertainment business," he told Mike.

"Mr. Williams, I'd love to work with them," Mike said.

The two chatted briefly and Pop left. Nearly a year later, he returned, this time with Leonard, Melvin, Doug, and Henry in tow. By then, Mike had joined forces with another lawyer and had moved his office downtown.

"Do you remember me?" he asked Mike.

"Of course I do, Mr. Williams."

"I wanted you to meet the boys," Pop said, then he paused. The look in his eye and the tone of his voice made Mike sit up and pay special attention.

Pop continued. "But before I introduce you to them, I want you to get one thing straight, man to man. If you become their lawyer, I want you to stay their lawyer and take care of them, forever."

At that point, Mike knew he had come into contact with an extraordinary man. "I will, Mr. Williams. I sure will," he answered.

More than a quarter century later, Mike Frascogna is still taking care of Pop's boys.

"Pop was a big strong man," Mike recalls. "You could tell he had grown up on a farm, doing hard physical labor all his life. And you could also tell that he loved his music and he loved his family. He probably didn't have much of a formal education but he was very intelligent. He knew the music business on a small basis at that time, but he also had enough sense to know there was a bigger, more complex arena out there that his boys would have to know how to move around in if they were to become successful. So, what he was doing was looking ahead and putting them together with a lawyer, someone who could help take care of them as they moved forward."

As tough as Pop was on his boys and others sometimes, he had a tender heart underneath his gruff exterior. When he saw potential in someone, he would do whatever it took to bring out the best in that person—but only if he saw that they were willing to work hard also. Dennis Tobias was one such individual.

Pop had been hosting a Sunday morning gospel music radio show at WAPF in McComb for a while. By the time The Williams Brothers started gaining national recognition in the early 1970s, Pop had made his radio program one of the most recognized of its kind in that area. He not only played Williams Brothers tunes but also paid attention to other national gospel groups.

When Pop came in to the radio station to record his program, he began taking notice of a young man who was producing his own gospel music program. Dennis Tobias was a high school student and budding musician from McComb who loved gospel music. He played in a local group and came up with the idea of doing a radio program that promoted local gospel groups and their music. The radio station bought the idea, so Dennis ended up at the station at the same time as Pop.

Pop noticed the young man's enthusiasm for his program and gradually took Dennis under his wing, explaining to him how he did certain things and why he did them that way. They spent many hours together in the studio, and as time passed, Dennis began to look up to Pop like a father. Dennis's home life had had its ups and downs and he was grateful for the guidance that came from a man like Leon Williams.

Dennis had grown up knowing about the Williams family and their music. As a young boy, he would put on a 45 record of "In My Dying Hours," one of The Williams Brothers early songs, and practice singing it and trying to figure out the music on his bass guitar.

"For any of us who were involved in gospel music around the McComb area, The Williams Brothers were the focal point of our education," says Dennis. "We looked at the path they had paved and how they handled themselves. They were very talented; that was obvious from just listening to the music they played and the songs they were writing. But Pop also kept them humble. He never let them think they were better than anyone else and he taught them to always consider the value of a human being. They are still that way today."

Just as the professionalism and style of The Williams Brothers had affected many would-be gospel musicians, these qualities rubbed off on Dennis Tobias. He could think of no other group that was better for him to emulate. And now, here he was, learning from the man who had made The Williams Brothers what they were.

After a few years of producing the two radio shows side by side—Dennis's program geared to the local scene and Pop's show more focused on national black gospel music led by The Williams Brothers—Pop started letting Dennis help him with his program. Dennis began doing some of the announcements and introducing some of the records for the show. Pop taught Dennis everything he knew about producing a gospel music radio program. Increasingly, he turned over responsibility to Dennis, and in 1975 they decided to merge the two shows into one.

As Pop saw that Dennis was able to handle each new task, he gave him more free rein. Eventually, Pop realized that the younger man could produce the radio show by himself. Dennis began learning more about actually promoting live gospel performances and even began to do some of the promoting for The Williams Brothers. He learned how to secure venues, locate and train spokespersons for the areas in which a concert was scheduled, buy and produce the newspaper ads and radio commercials for concerts, distribute flyers, and make live radio appearances on behalf of the group.

Throughout his years as a college student at Alcorn State University, Dennis continued to work closely with Pop. After Dennis married and started a family, his wife and children were practically adopted by Mom and Pop Williams, who treated them like their own grandchildren. Some of Dennis's fondest memories from his twin sons' early days were of them loading up into Pop's truck for a summertime fishing trip with their "Big Daddy."

Not only did Pop teach Dennis about the music business, he taught him a lot about handling life. "To describe Pop Williams is to say he was a man. He did whatever he had to do to provide for his family, no matter how many hours it took. He worked hard, and expected everyone else to work hard around him. His strength came from the Lord, however, and if, after he had worked hard and done whatever he could to make something happened, it failed, then he would say 'That's the Lord's will and we have to accept that and go on and do something else.' Pop would always say that there must be something better in store from the Lord," Dennis remembers.

Dennis would apply the truth and comfort of Pop's philosophy of life when one day his newly built home burned to the ground and it seemed that the payoff on the mortgage for the house was more than the insurance money could cover. Dennis came close to despair, but was eventually able to use Pop's words to set his mind at ease. Truly believing that there was "something better in store from the Lord," Dennis turned back to the routine of his daily life. And things did work out. Incredibly, he found a contractor who built a house almost twice as big as the original one for nearly the same price.

"Pop always seemed to be able to see through clouds to the silver lining. I learned how to do that, from watching him," Dennis said.

Today, Dennis and his family live in Fernwood and he continues to produce a gospel music radio show for WAKK in McComb. He keeps up with the Williams family and still visits Mom Williams at The Big House in Smithdale. Not surprisingly, he pays special attention—in terms of production and instrumental and vocal arrangements—to the songs that come out by The Williams Brothers. In his opinion, in the world of gospel music, there is no better example than these local boys who made good. He also manages a young gospel group patterned after The Williams Brothers, The Christianaires.

1973-1990

OVERLEAF, AND RIGHT: *The photograph on the preceding page, taken in 1973 in front of a medical clinic in Bude, Mississippi, shows (from left to right): Maurice Surrell, Melvin Williams, Doug Williams, Leonard Williams, and Henry Green. The same group, in the same place and on the same day, is shown here posing in front of their tour van.*

ABOVE: *Four years later, in 1977, the lineup is the same (from left to right, Henry, Maurice, Leonard, Melvin, and Doug), but the look is very different.*

Amanda and Pop Williams with Cliff Finch, then Governor of Mississippi. The photograph was taken in McComb, in 1975.

Christmas at The Big House, 1978. From left to right, Marilyn, Deliana, and Josie Marie.

78

This studio photo, taken in 1978, shows three generations of the Williams family: From left to right: granddaughter Amanda Banks Gary (Anthony Gary is Amanda's second husband), Mom Williams, granddaughter Linder Banks Williams, cousins Sheila Ramsey Wells and Margie Ramsey Hughes, and four of Mom's children, Deliana, Marilyn, Frank, and Josie Marie.

ABOVE, LEFT: *This photo, snapped at the Soul Train Music Awards in 1987, shows (left to right) the Reverend Andraé Crouch, Ron Winans, and Melvin Williams.*

ABOVE, RIGHT: *Taken shortly before Pop Williams' death, this photograph shows Leon Sr. with Dennis Tobias, holding The Williams Brothers' 1989 album* Ain't Love Wonderful. *Tobias, who was one of Pop's protégés, currently produces a gospel music radio show for WAKK in McComb and manages The Christianaires, a well-known gospel quartet. Doug and Melvin Williams worked with The Christianaires on their 1996 album* Saints Hold On.

ABOVE LEFT: *The Jackson Southernaires, in about 1990. From left to right, front row: Maurice Surrell, Frank Williams, James Burks. From left to right, back row: Grenard McClendon, Gary Myers, Melvin Wilson, Huey Williams, and Roger Bryant.* ABOVE RIGHT: *Willie Banks, in a studio shot taken about 1989. Banks sang with The Jackson Southernaires in the late 1960s, and later formed a gospel group of his own, Willie Banks and The Messengers. Deliana Williams married Willie Banks in 1954; they were divorced in 1973.*

LEFT, ABOVE AND BELOW: *After Leonard Williams left, in 1988, The Williams Brothers became a gospel trio: Doug Williams, Melvin Williams, and Henry Green. The top photo was taken at Tom Joynt's Photography Studio in Jackson in 1989. In the bottom photo, taken at City Auditorium in Valdosta, Georgia, in 1990, are (left to right), Melvin and Doug Williams, Henry Green, and Terrell "Midge" Gatlin, long-time backup musician for various incarnations of The Williams Brothers.*

CHAPTER VII   Frank's Story

Just standing there with her shy
smile, in her best Sunday dress
with her knee socks and patent
leather shoes, Ayannah has
already captured the hearts of
the entire congregation at Rose
Hill this night. Now, she will
melt those hearts.

Taking the microphone, with soft keyboard notes floating in the background, she
whispers, "This is for my uncle Frank."

Then she begins the song "Come by Here, Dear Lord."

> Come by here, Dear Lord, Come by here.
> Oh Lord, come by here.
> Someone's crying, Lord, Come by here.
> Someone's praying, Lord, Come by here.
> Oh Lord, come by here.

Tears well up in eyes throughout the room. Out in the hallway, Doug feels his
throat tighten as his daughter sings the song his brother Frank has always loved.

Mom Williams smiles and looks back at her daughter-in-law Katrina, who has

driven down from Jackson for the concert with her children Theja, Jessica, and Frankie.
Three-year-old Frankie turns and smiles back at his grandmother, warming her heart.
He looks so much like his father Frank when he was that age, so full of life and curiosity.

Ayannah finishes her song with a smile and the choir immediately moves into another
hymn. Lillian Lilly steps forward to sing. Though she is short in stature, her voice fills
the room. She is a soloist for the renowned Mississippi Mass Choir, which was founded
by Frank Williams. With two brief selections, she brings the audience to its feet, swaying
to the music, clapping and raising their hands to the Lord.

Frank would love this, Amanda thought, if he were here at the church tonight.

When the children played church, little Frank never hesitated to play the
role of the preacher. Sure, he would join in and sing as a member of the mock
choir with his brothers and sisters. But when it was preaching time out there in
the yard, he was the preacher.

Amanda watched the children through the window. That little Frank. Such
a serious child, she thought, like a little man. The other children would tease
him sometimes. But not too much. There was something about the boy—
his quiet manner and his confidence in the abilities the Lord had given him.
It seemed that from the time he was a baby, he knew exactly what he wanted
and he always looked to the Lord to provide him direction.

Not that he wasn't a hard-headed child sometimes. He and Josie Marie, the
sister who was five years older, were close buddies. With such a large family,
the older children were expected to take the younger ones under their wings,
and, yes, even deliver punishment in their parents' absence, if the misdeed
warranted discipline.

Frank and Josie Marie had butted heads on occasion as older sister tried
to keep her younger brother in line. Their mother was of the opinion that
maybe Marie enjoyed her position of power a little too much. "One day he
will get bigger and stronger than you, and you will not be able to bully him,"

Amanda would tell Marie. Sure enough, Marie was trying to drag Frank in a direction he didn't want to go one day, and he simply put a bear hug on his older sister until she was immobilized. And that, Marie would later laughingly say, was the beginning of the next phase of their relationship, one where their roles were ultimately reversed, where she—along with many others—would look to Frank for guidance and comfort.

Frank discovered his musical talent early, and was singing beautiful solos in church by the time he was 5. He also learned to play guitar and piano when he was still quite young, and as soon as he could write, was creating his own little songs. Though he was the youngest of the group of Williams brothers and sisters that made up the Southern Gospel Singers, his thoughtful nature and natural leadership ability made it logical for the others to include him when decisions were to be made for the group. Frank had a rare combination of abilities. He was a true artist, and created some of the most moving gospel music people had ever heard. At the same time, he possessed a keen administrative sense and was able to coordinate efforts toward a common goal, and in times to come, people around Frank would look to him to make organizational decisions.

Frank never shirked the duties required of him in the family and would work his turn in the fields with everyone else. In the summers, he worked alongside his father laying brick, just like his brothers did. But, where big brother Bill saw a career as a brick contractor ahead, Frank had other dreams.

"I am going to work in an office," the pint-sized middle child announced one day to the rest of the family. "I'm going to go to college and then I will have an office of my own somewhere." Somehow, they knew that if little Frank said it, it would become reality.

Frank left home to attend Jackson State University. While in college, he started singing with The Jackson Southernaires, becoming a featured singer on their albums. Frank had followed brother Huey in joining the group, a men's gospel quartet. One of the other members of The Jackson Southernaires was Willie Banks, husband of sister Deliana, with whom both Frank and Huey lived while in Jackson. The quartet, originally called The Shaw Southernaires because they received sponsorship and their uniforms from Shaw's Department Store in Jackson, was renamed once it had became one of Malaco Records' most successful gospel groups. It was in Jackson that Huey introduced Frank to Dorothy Jean Kennebrew. After graduating from JSU with degrees in Music and Business Administration, Frank married Dorothy Jean and settled down to work at Malaco Records in their gospel music division. He had that office he had always said he would get some day.

The family was always part of his thinking, however, and he decided that the women of the Williams clan needed a showcase for their talents, too. In the early 1980s, he formed a group that he simply called The Williams Family. Frank sang with the group, but other members were all female: his mother Amanda; his sisters Deliana, Josie Marie, and Marilyn; Deliana's daughters Amanda and Linder; and cousins Margie and Sheila Ramsey. The two albums made by the Williams Family were released by Malaco Records.

In late 1985, as Frank was seeing some of his dreams come to life, a terrible blow was delivered. His beloved wife Dorothy died of cancer, leaving Frank with their nine-year-old daughter Theja. Although the tragic loss shook Frank to his core, it did not crush his spirit. Instead, it gave him cause to reexamine his calling, to return to something he had first thought about several years earlier. A larger vision had been tugging at him for a while and the time was drawing near for it to become reality. In the next few years, the Lord basically reset Frank's priorities.

Several months after Dorothy passed away, Frank was introduced by Stewart Madison, a co-owner of Malaco Records, to a young lady named Katrina Belton, a speech pathologist at Methodist Rehabilitation Center in

Jackson. Katrina, ten years younger than Frank, remembered him from the days of her childhood in Vicksburg, Mississippi, when she and her sisters sold tickets at the door for Jackson Southernaire concerts. They met for lunch and discovered they shared many interests. In January 1986, they were married.

Frank looked at the faces around his and Katrina's dining room table: Jerry Mannery, assistant and understudy of Frank's at Malaco; the Reverend Benjamin Cone, originally from Waycross, Georgia, a powerful preacher and longtime friend; Jerry Smith; David Curry, well-known musician in the Jackson area; Roy Wooten, national promotions director for Malaco; and the Reverend Milton Biggham, founder of The Georgia Mass Choir and executive at Savoy Records in New York (later a division of Malaco). They all looked at Frank's face on this spring night in 1988 and knew what he wanted to talk about. He had that look again.

For several years they had heard Frank talk about his vision, a dream he felt he was destined to realize: a mass choir with a new sound. They had gathered around the table with Frank many times to talk about it.

Frank sat at the head of the table and looked at his close friends and associates. On the wall behind him hung several of the industry awards he had been given as a producer, performer, songwriter, and director of the Malaco Gospel Division.

"No more talking," he announced. "I want to form the choir."

As often as he had talked about forming a special multiracial, nondenominational choir, they knew this time it was different. Frank had a mission and he was ready now to see it through; like Moses in the Bible, he had faced his fears and was ready to meet the challenge that God had put before him.

The first board of directors for the new Mississippi Mass Choir was formed around that table. David Curry, from Frank's home church in Jackson, would be Minister of Music. Frank would not have it any other way than for Reverend Cone to be the choir's spiritual advisor. Cone's daughter was a big fan of The Jackson Southernaires.

Frank had first met Reverend Cone one day when the Reverend came into the Malaco office to return a defective Jackson Southernaires record. Frank happened to be standing at the receptionist's desk and the two men started talking. Frank and Reverend Cone became instant friends and there was many a night in the months ahead when they made the time in their busy schedules to discuss the Lord and the Scriptures.

The two made for a study in contrasts: Frank with his slender frame and soft-spoken manner, and the taller, heavy-set Cone with his booming, larger-than-life bass voice. They had one thing in common that outweighed all differences, and that was a profound love of the Gospel. It wasn't unusual for them to spend hours talking about the Bible, and soon Frank began asking Cone to advise the groups the record company was signing. When it came time to choose someone for that same position with the mass choir, there was no other choice for Frank.

The morning after that dining table meeting, Frank asked Roy Wooten to help him get the word out about the choir. They decided on a media blitz. Announcements were sent to daily and rural newspapers, television stations, radio stations. Hardly a soul in Mississippi didn't know that Frank Williams was forming a choir, and hundreds of tapes started pouring into the Malaco offices from across the state.

Next came the hard part: selecting those who would be asked to come to Jackson for auditions. Frank and his board found themselves once again gathered around the dining room table, listening to every tape. Those chosen for an audition had to demonstrate not only musical excellence but a dedication to the Lord and a desire to live for Him.

Eventually, all the auditions were held and 125 members were selected, among them his wife Katrina, his sisters Marilyn and Deliana, and Deliana's daughters Linder and Amanda. The board was in unanimous agreement that Frank Williams would be the main lead singer for the choir.

The first rehearsal was to be a monumental event.

All eyes were on Frank as he explained exactly the sound he wanted. "We're going to try something new," he said. "We're going to sing with the spirit and energy of a quartet, and the strength and volume of many."

The sound was inspiring. The practice sessions during the next few months weren't so much rehearsals as they were devotionals and outright worship services in their own right.

Before each of the sessions, Frank would ask Reverend Cone or one of the other advisors to lead the group in prayer. Sometimes he would lead the group in prayer also. Then, for the next three hours, there would be such joy in the singing that it seemed every body would be filled with the Spirit and every voice would resound more fully and loudly than it ever had before.

It was obvious to everyone that something very special was happening at the rehearsals. But how would it be with a live audience? To find out, Frank scheduled two warm-up concerts.

The first was on a breezy early summer night in the tiny north Mississippi town of Belden. For weeks before the concert, members of the choir from that area had been talking about the group and its new sound. There wasn't an empty seat in the house when the choir performed. The audience wasn't disappointed. They were on their feet clapping and singing along before the choir finished the first number.

The second warm-up was a little closer to home. The city auditorium was booked in Vicksburg, forty miles west of Jackson on the Mississippi River. Word had spread quickly after the Belden concert, and the 500-seat auditorium was overflowing as people stood in the aisles to hear gospel music like they had never heard it before.

Frank concluded both concerts the same way: "Make plans to join The Mississippi Mass Choir at the Jackson Municipal Auditorium in November and help them celebrate as they record their first album. Come and share the Spirit of the Lord with us."

Everyone must have taken his words as a personal invitation because the night of the recording, all 2,700 seats in the auditorium were filled. Judging from the number who were turned away at the door, it could have been filled again. Those who couldn't get inside stood around and sat on the steps on the front of the auditorium, just to say they had been there the night of "the recording."

On the far side of the building, a few enterprising fans found a door that was propped open by some recording cables and stood there waiting for the concert to begin, content to listen from outside.

Backstage, choir members spent the few minutes before the recording warming up their voices and trying to deal with the mammoth-sized butterflies that were building inside. Technicians scurried from the microphones on stage to the sound boards, getting last minute sound checks, then double- and triple-checking cable connections.

The recording would not begin until Frank said so. Not surprisingly, he was the calming influence for the entire event. He knew everything would work out fine. After all, this was what was supposed to be happening this night, and he was doing what he was called to do.

A few technical glitches held up the concert, but twenty minutes after it was scheduled to start, Frank nodded his head. It was time.

Choir members shifted nervously in position and smoothed their robes. Frank asked Reverend Cone to lead the choir in prayer. Then he nodded to his technicians and the house lights went down. Anticipation that had been building in the audience suddenly erupted like thunder as a spontaneous burst of applause greeted the choir. The curtain slowly rose and the stage lights pulsed on to illuminate The Mississippi Mass Choir.

The music began and the choir started to sing "Having You There."

We have come to praise and magnify the Lord
For all that He has done and for the victory we have won.
In the good times and in the bad times,
In the happy times and in the sad times,
Having You there, made the difference,
Just having You there, Having You there.

I thank You for Your mercy, I thank You for Your grace.
There is no other one who can ever take Your place.
When my friends walked out, You stepped right in.
You've always been with me through the thick and the thin.
Having You there, made the difference,
*Just having You there, Having You there.**

The song summed up Frank's relationship with God and his feeling for the music and ministry vision for the Mass Choir. For the next three hours, the recording session proceeded flawlessly.

The evening was inspired. Neither Frank nor the choir had ever been in better voice. Now not only would the Jackson Municipal Auditorium be known as the American host of the International Ballet Competition, it would be known as the birthplace of the recordings of The Mississippi Mass Choir.

Frank's work was just beginning, however. The album had to be prepared for a June 1989 release. As he worked in the studio, the choir continued its rehearsals and started making concert appearances throughout the state.

*   *Written by D.R. Curry, Jr. © 1989 Malaco Music.*

When the album was released, the music industry—and the entire country, for that matter—enthusiastically embraced the "choirtet" sound and what many considered the special "anointing" of the choir. Six weeks after the *Mississippi Mass Choir Live* album was released it went to number one on the Billboard Gospel chart. In another six weeks it was *Cash Box Magazine*'s number one gospel album in the nation.

It stayed at the summit of both charts for 11 months. For 42 weeks it topped *Billboard*'s chart, slipped to number two briefly, then rose back to the top spot.

Recognition and honors flowed to the choir. The week-long James Cleveland Gospel Music Workshop of America honored the choir as Choir of the Year—Traditional and as the Best New Artist of the Year. At the 1989 Stellar Awards for gospel music, the choir swept the major categories, taking home awards for Choir of the Year, Album of the Year, Best New Artist, and Best Gospel Video. Nominations also came in from the Dove Awards and the Soul Train Music Awards.

Individually, Frank was to be singled out as Producer of the Year by the Gospel Announcers Guild, and in 1990 he received the Governor's Award for Excellence in the Arts.

Everyone wanted to see and hear The Mississippi Mass Choir. Concert requests began flooding the choir's office from all over the world. Filling those requests took the choir across the country to perform in large auditoriums, small churches, and outdoor venues of all types. To gospel fans, it didn't seem to matter where or when the choir sang. They just wanted to hear them. No matter where they went, though, Frank insisted that they begin and end each performance with prayer.

Often when they traveled, choir members were asked to sing. They could hardly board an airplane without being asked for a mini-concert. Restaurant owners would literally ask them to sing for their supper. And then there was that impromptu concert in front of a popular restaurant on Bourbon Street in New Orleans.

About twenty choir members were walking back to their hotel after a meal when they stopped to listen to a man playing a saxophone for tips. He asked the group at large if they were part of a convention and, upon learning they were part of a gospel choir, he broke into a traditional gospel number. One choir member started singing as he played, then another, and then another until the entire group was singing on the street corner normally reserved for the single musician. Tourists began gathering and dropping bills into the street musician's open saxophone case. With that one song, he filled the case.

What had to be the strangest performance came on a return trip from a concert. Driving through Alabama toward Jackson early one morning, the driver of the choir's tour bus noticed that a pickup truck coming from the opposite direction had U-turned and was now following the bus. The man in the pickup began honking and waving as he pulled alongside the bus. By now, most of the choir was awake and staring out of the windows at the man. Some started waving at him, and finally they decided to pull over, since he didn't seem threatening.

"Are you really, really The Mississippi Mass Choir?" he asked them when a few of the men stepped down from the bus to greet him. "Yes we are," they answered.

"I have your album. You people are incredible!" he said, visibly excited. "I was coming to your concert but I had to go out of town on a job and missed it. I can't believe it is really you. Please, please would you sing something for me?" The man was practically begging.

Not wanting to disappoint any of their fans, the choir piled out of the bus and lined up on the side of the interstate highway. The man took a seat on the bed of his pickup as the choir sang two a capella numbers for him. When they were finished, he came over to them with tears in his eyes and shook hands with every choir member.

The Mississippi Mass Choir sang in all types of situations, from impromptu roadsides to *The Today Show,* but occasionally they were reminded that the Lord loved humility.

On the way back from Washington, D.C., after a performance scheduled for President Clinton had been cancelled due to irregularities in a parade schedule, the bus carrying the choir broke down in Virginia. Although a state trooper came by minutes later, he was unable to locate a vehicle large enough for the group. Finally he found something for them.

"I'm sorry," he said, "but the only thing I can find is a prison transport bus. It's got bars on the windows, but it is warm and it'll get you into town while they work on your tour bus."

Half an hour later, they were peeking at the passing countryside through the bars on the bus windows. First, the cancelled presidential performance, now this, they thought.

"It's the Lord's way of keeping us humble and grounded," Frank told them. "He wanted to remind us of what's important before we record the new album."

"Amen," the choir answered him.

Four days after the choir returned to Jackson, The Mississippi Mass Choir began working on its new album. The recording session would be one the choir members would never forget and one of Frank's finest performances.

CHAPTER VIII

Through Good Times... and Through Low Times

Thomas Saulsberry walks up to the front of the church and strikes the pose he always uses when introducing the group.

The audience is buzzing now. Almost, almost, almost. . .just a few more minutes.

Doug, Melvin, and Henry are pacing now, ready for Thomas, the director of promotions and marketing for Blackberry Records, to start talking.

"Normally when I stand up here and do this, I would start something like this," Thomas says, putting on his booming professional announcer voice, "Allllll the way from SMITHDALE, MISSISSIPPI."

The crowd laughs.

"But I can't do that tonight," he says, "so why don't we change it." He switches to announcer voice again, "Let's. . .welcome. . .home. . . THE WILLIAMS BROTHERS!!"

The congregation is on its feet now as Doug and Melvin lead the group out on the run. The ovation is deafening. A voice in the back calls out, "Welcome home!"

In his purple, black, and white suit, Melvin stops, looks at Doug, then turns to acknowledge the greeting with a big grin. The music starts.

With their very first note, the group begins to take the church on a spiritual journey that will last for two hours, the effect of which is nothing short of phenomenal.

When she heard the room full of people burst into the song "Happy Birthday," Amanda tried to back out of the door she had just walked into.

"We've interrupted someone's party," she told her middle son Frank. Frank didn't say a word as he gently guided his mother into the banquet room at the McComb Holiday Inn on a September evening in 1977.

As she looked around the room, Amanda began to recognize a few faces. Why, her other children were here. Marilyn, Doug, Melvin, Deliana, Huey, Leonard, and Leon Jr. Then it hit her. They weren't just singing to someone, they were singing to her! Tears of joy trickled down her cheeks as she thought of all the trouble Pop and the kids had gone to, just to plan this surprise party for her. She immediately began hugging everyone she could get her hands on.

The room was decorated beautifully with bright flower arrangements in the middle of every table and balloons with streamers tied to every chair. Yes, her family had pulled a fast one on her. She should have sensed it from how strange Frank was acting. He and Dorothy Jean had driven down from Jackson, telling her and Pop to hurry up and get dressed because they had reservations to take them out to dinner for Mom's birthday. But after Amanda and Pop had rushed frantically to get ready, Frank had started making excuses for why they couldn't leave yet. Amanda had gotten exasperated with her son, who was usually such a stickler for being punctual. For some reason she couldn't explain, he didn't mind being late tonight.

When they finally arrived at the Holiday Inn, they were told they would have to wait in the lobby. Frank hopped up every few minutes like a jumping bean, rushing back and forth to check on the banquet hall. Finally they were led to the room, but still Amanda didn't suspect a thing, not until the second chorus of "Happy Birthday" rang out.

For the rest of the evening, it was like Amanda was holding court. Two of the large tables had been pushed together and the entire family had gathered around—sons and daughters and their spouses and all the grandchildren—

all the family in one place. Even Josie Marie, who was still living in California at the time, was there.

To Amanda, having her entire family around her was the best birthday present anyone could have given her. All night long friends and other relatives crowded around her table to pass along their best wishes. Amanda made a point of thanking each of them for being there and making her birthday so special.

She talked to so many people that night, they soon became a blur, which was why when one of her sisters-in-law, Victoria Ridley, kept coming up to the table excitedly exclaiming "They got you a new...," it didn't register with her. And each time Victoria came close, Pop or one of the kids could steer her away quickly, but Amanda didn't notice that either.

The party finally wound down and Pop and the kids helped Amanda gather her gifts. "Frank, why don't you bring your car around so we can put the gifts in it?" she asked her son. Frank nodded and left the room, only to return too quickly, it seemed, to have brought the car all the way from the front of the hotel.

With the girls leading the way, Amanda's army made its way to the front door. Deliana and Marilyn held the door open for her and Pop.

And there it was.

Fortunately, Huey and Doug were right behind Amanda, because when she saw that brand new tan Chrysler Cordova with a huge red ribbon on top of it, her knees buckled and she broke into tears. Her sons caught her before she hit the floor.

Hugging his mother tightly, Doug laughed and said, "We won't have to push this one into the woods either. It's all yours." The Williamses all knew exactly what Doug was talking about. They broke into laughter at the memory of the times they had to push Pop's car into the woods and cover it with brush and twigs to hide from the repo man.

Amanda hugged Doug but she couldn't get the words out to tell him that she remembered those times too. She was speechless and just smiled at her children with tears on her face. She cried with happiness all the way home.

As with every family, there were peaks and valleys. In 1989, the Williams family dipped into the lowest valley they had known.

Pop Williams, though still in good health, had stopped traveling with The Williams Brothers by the mid-'80s, leaving the rigors of the road for the younger men. He was still active though, and when the roof needed repairing he swung into action. On September 6, 1989, he had been pounding on the roof all morning long. Amanda knew how long he had been up there because she could hear every nail being driven. Even at 79, Pop could still swing a mean hammer.

Then the hammering stopped. Pop came down off the ladder and into the house.

"I've got to go into town for some more two-by-fours and materials," he said. He kissed her cheek and, as he always did, poked one of his callused fingers into the middle of a pie she had just set out to cool. Grinning at her, he dodged the dish towel she was trying to swat him with and walked out to his truck. He drove down Williams Brothers Road to the highway, honking at Aunt Nez, who was sitting on her front porch shelling peas.

At West Building Materials in McComb, he spent only ten minutes getting the lumber and roofing shingles he needed, and another thirty minutes talking with the guys in the lumber yard, catching up on all that was going on with their families. Then he got back in his truck, drove out to Interstate 55 at the Presley Boulevard exit, and started north toward home.

He hadn't gotten very far when he noticed an 18-wheeler bearing down on him. The 24-year-old driver of the semi was hauling eighty 55-gallon drums of liquid plastic to Illinois.

Pop looked in his rear view mirror again just as he passed the Park Drive overpass, thinking that the driver of the truck would change lanes any second now to pass him. But he didn't.

The 18-wheeler ran right over Pop's pickup truck, dragging it 150 feet down the interstate highway. The roofing shingles went flying from the bed of the pickup and the two-by-four boards were driven straight through the cab.

Pop died instantly.

The clock in the pickup stopped at 12:30 p.m.

A mile away, Henry Green was having lunch at the Holiday Inn with some out-of-town cousins. The group hardly noticed the sound of sirens in the distance. "Must have been an accident," Henry said. They were just finishing their meal when Henry noticed a friend, a volunteer firefighter, enter the restaurant.

"Green, can I see you outside a minute," his friend said.

A cold knot formed in Henry's stomach when he saw the look on the man's face. "What is it?" he said when the two had walked out to the parking lot.

"It's Pop, man," the friend said.

Henry was finding it hard to breathe. He stared at the man.

"I'm sorry. He's dead."

Henry couldn't say anything for a minute. "This is some kind of joke. "

"I wish it were. There was an 18-wheeler just up the highway. He didn't have. . . ."

Henry didn't wait for his friend to finish. He bolted toward the interstate, running in the direction his friend had pointed.

"Green, wait!" The friend caught up with Henry a couple of hundred yards away and led him back to his pickup to take him to the accident site.

By the time they got there the ambulance had already left for Southwest Regional Medical Center in McComb. Henry stood there staring in disbelief at the twisted and crumpled pickup. Maybe if he stared at it hard enough the wreckage would go away and Pop would be all right.

"If only the lumber hadn't been in the back of the truck, he might have survived," a nearby highway patrolman said.

"Wonder why he stopped in the middle of the interstate?" another asked.

By the time Amanda and Marilyn arrived at the hospital, Doug, Melvin, and Henry were already there. Doug was in the corner talking to a police officer. Melvin came over to them immediately, and they sat close together in the tiny waiting room. Doug joined them. "I don't believe it," he said. "They're saying Pop stopped his truck in the middle of the interstate."

Just then, an attendant came up and said they were ready for the identification of the body. Doug stepped forward. "I'll do it." Seeing Pop like that was not how he wanted his mother to remember his father and her husband of more than 50 years, the only man she had ever been with.

By the time everyone had arrived home from the hospital, word had spread throughout the community. People were bringing food and offering their help. Frank and Leonard made it down from Jackson in record time. Amanda knew she wouldn't make it through the next few days if it weren't for her children. Hundreds of calls and letters came in, and the Craft Funeral Home reserved two rooms to hold all the flowers that had been sent from literally all over the world.

Frank, Doug, and Marilyn took care of making the funeral arrangements. Pop had always said he wanted to be buried at his home church at Rose Hill, and that is what they planned.

But there was something else Doug needed to do. He did not believe the official report that stated his father was killed because he had stopped his truck in the middle of the interstate. Henry felt the same way, so the two of them took off to talk to anyone who might have seen the accident. They had a list of witnesses from the Highway Patrol and talked to each of them. One by one, the witnesses remembered that Pop hadn't actually stopped on the highway; he had just been driving very slowly.

"I told the guy I was riding with," said one man, "that big truck is going to run over that pickup and sure enough, he did; he didn't even slow down."

Doug uncovered another disturbing fact from the Highway Patrol report. The driver of the 18-wheeler wasn't even going to be charged, despite the fact that his log book had been altered. The official log book of the truck driver said he had pulled out of Hammond, Louisiana, some 60 miles south of McComb, at 1 p.m., 30 minutes after the accident had occurred. Even though Doug knew he would have questions about the accident for the rest of his life, at least he knew that his father had not been responsible.

It was a warm September afternoon when Leon "Pop" Williams, Sr. was laid to rest.

The Reverend Al Green drove down from Memphis to pay his respects and sing at the funeral. It was the least he could do for Pop, after all the times Pop had brought him to The Big House for one of Amanda's home-cooked meals. Reverend Green, like everyone else, knew the Williams family home as The Big House because despite its smallness there was always love enough and room enough for one more person, whoever it might be who walked through the door.

Everyone who knew and loved Pop was there. It didn't take long for the tiny red-brick Rose Hill Missionary Baptist Church to fill. Nearly 300 people sat shoulder to shoulder inside the church, and four times that many gathered outside. Friends and acquaintances, national recording artists and announcers, all were there, peering through the windows or through the petals of the flower arrangements that lined both sides of the sanctuary three-deep. More flowers surrounded Pop's casket at the front of the church, forming a blanket of love and support for the entire family.

Amanda was still in shock for most of the service, grateful that her children were taking charge. They were all there by her side when Reverend Ricky Carter began the service by praising Pop and all the work he had done for the church. When Al Green started to sing "The Lord Will Make a Way Somehow," his voice cracked with emotion, but the family drew strength from the words. How true they were. The Lord would help them get through this. Somehow.

Amanda sat for two and a half hours, until every person inside and out had made his or her way down the short aisle to say a final farewell to Pop.

The flowers that would not fit inside the church had already been placed in the cemetery around Pop's freshly dug grave. He would be lying right next to his mother in the family plot. What flowers weren't around his grave would go around hers.

After the ceremony, Amanda was exhausted, but she knew close friends and the rest of the family would be coming by The Big House. The tiny kitchen was filled with food, and the house was soon filled with warm and funny memories of Pop.

Deliana and Huey remembered the many times Pop had tried to ride their stubborn old mule Diamond, only to be bucked off into the pond. And how one day Pop had finally had enough and whacked Diamond on the nose with a hammer.

Doug thought of the time Pop had slipped a disc while on a bricklaying job and had to spend two weeks in St. Dominic Hospital in Jackson. The younger children hadn't been allowed to visit, and when Pop finally came home, little Doug ran and jumped in his lap and wouldn't move for about two hours.

Frank started singing softly the song he and Deliana had been singing while playing church in the yard, when Pop pulled him in and formed the Southern Gospel Singers.

Josie Marie smiled, thinking that when they were kids, they knew that anytime Pop came in from town, his pockets would be filled with "silver bell" chocolate candies.

As the memories unfolded they realized that Pop hadn't left them forever.

He had just gone on to prepare the foundation for the next home his family would have in Heaven.

It was hard for Doug, Melvin, and Henry to get out of bed that next Monday morning. Usually, Pop would give them each a morning wake-up call by six or seven. But no call came that morning. And the absence of that call reminded them that he was really gone.

"Maybe we should take some time off," Henry suggested. Doug and Melvin weren't sure that was a good idea.

Deep inside, each of them were wondering how they were going to make it through their next performance, which was scheduled for the following weekend in the little north Mississippi town of Pickens.

"Maybe we should cancel," Doug finally said.

For hours they talked and prayed about what they should do, yet they couldn't make up their minds. They were caught in a fog of misery and sadness. Suddenly a question formed in Doug's mind, and he said it aloud.

"What would Pop do. . .or what would he want us to do?"

They all knew what the answer was, and all three said it out loud. "He'd want us to sing."

The following Saturday night, The Williams Brothers stood in front of a small crowd in the Pickens High School Auditorium. Melvin took a deep breath and stepped up to the microphone.

"For you, Pop," he said. And then they sang "Jesus Will Fix It."

> *I know that Jesus will fix it for you,*
> *For He knows just what to do.*
> *Whenever you pray, just let Him have His way.*
> *Oh! Jesus, he will fix it all by and by.'*
>
> *Whenever you have problems, and your best friends just can't be found,*
> *Fall down on your knees, call on Jesus.*

He'll never, never, never let you down.
Oh! Jesus, he will fix it all by and by.

All by and by,
He'll fix it for you."*

It was one of the most difficult performances they would ever have to do, but it was also one of the best because they knew in their hearts that Pop would want it that way. They could imagine Pop sitting in the front row of the auditorium, tapping his feet, his arms raised, swaying and smiling as they sang.

---

* | *Arrangement by Doug Williams and Melvin Williams. © 1999 Dalf Music / Melvin Williams Music.*

1991–1998

OVERLEAF: *Melvin Williams in 1994 at the Jubilee Jam, in Jackson Mississippi, an annual event that attracts a diverse roster of musicians. Performing with The Williams Brothers that year were Little Richard, The Neville Brothers, Slim and the The Supreme Angels, and The Jackson Southernaires.*

RIGHT: *A summer day in 1993, in front of Doug Williams' house. At the extreme left are Melvin and Franklin Delano Jr. (Frank and Katrina's son); left to right after Melvin are Deliana, Josie Marie, Huey, Amanda, Marilyn, and Doug.*

ABOVE, LEFT: *Inmates at the Allen Correctional Institute in Lima, Ohio, lifting up their hands in praise and unity at a Williams Brothers concert in 1997.* ABOVE, RIGHT: *A spontaneous gospel trio formed when Melvin joined in with two inmates.*

RIGHT: *Ayannah Williams (Doug and Lavannah's daughter) with gospel great Kirk Franklin in December 1997 at the nominee reception for the Stellar Awards in Nashville.*

A few selected shots of the Williams family—and extended family. Clockwise from top left: Terralesia (Leon Jr. and Ruth's daughter) and Julian Thompson, Christmas at The Big House 1996; Theja (Frank and Dorothy Jean's daughter) and Fred Quin, Christmas at The Big House 1997; Jessica (Frank and Katrina's daughter) at age 6 (1993); Fumiko and Magan Beauchamp Seymore in 1997; and Paige Michael Williams at age 4 (1992).

ABOVE: *The Rose Hill Missionary Baptist Church, where the Williams family has worshipped for decades, where generations of Williams children have sung in the choir, where Leon Williams, Sr., is buried. The Family Night concert described at the beginning of each chapter was held at the Rose Hill Church on October 17, 1993.*

LEFT: *Mom Williams standing inside The Big House in Smithdale, built in 1940–1941, which has welcomed four generations of Williamses and their husbands and wives, children, and friends. All the exterior brickwork for the house was done by Leon Sr., Leon Jr., and Huey. The fancy interior brickwork, like the curved section shown here that does double duty as a console and trophy case, was done by Leon Sr.*

Aunt Nez in 1997. Inez Jackson became a second mother to all the Williams children after moving to Smithdale in 1951, and has been a second grandmother and great-grandmother to succeeding generations.

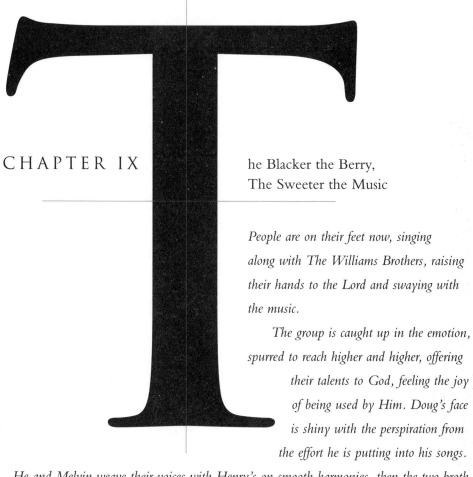

CHAPTER IX

he Blacker the Berry,
The Sweeter the Music

*People are on their feet now, singing
along with The Williams Brothers, raising
their hands to the Lord and swaying with
the music.*

*The group is caught up in the emotion,
spurred to reach higher and higher, offering
their talents to God, feeling the joy
of being used by Him. Doug's face
is shiny with the perspiration from
the effort he is putting into his songs.*

He and Melvin weave their voices with Henry's on smooth harmonies, then the two brothers erupt into the lead vocals, alternately taking the lead, then giving it back. As much as they have ever felt the Lord's presence in their music, they feel His Spirit moving tonight.

And the crowd feels it too.

Unabashedly the worshippers wave their hands toward heaven, shouting "Amen!" to punctuate the music. Some even dance with joy as the music takes them to a place where dancing for the Lord is the only thing they can do at that moment.

Everywhere people are standing, singing, clapping. It could easily be mistaken for a rock concert, except this is not rock and roll. This is gospel and those who haven't experienced it before will always remember the outpouring of faith and love.

This is what the years of work at their music have produced for The Williams Brothers: A sound and a message that pierces hearts and touches souls for the God they worship. To make this music is simply an act of obedience for them, yet they could never have imagined that obeying could bring such sweet fulfillment.

From the time they were youngsters, the Williamses had heard their father's little rules for life. Leon Williams was an independent man; he never wanted to depend on someone else if he could do it himself. One of his slogans was "Have Your Own."

Mike Frascogna notes that even before Pop's passing, the "boys" began honing the skills that would allow them to "have their own" as business people:

"Doug is very laid back, but in a very positive way. Diplomatic, a good businessman, he would do well in any business he decided to do, whether he was an accountant or a store owner.

"Melvin is extremely personable and has the same diplomatic manner, but in a different way. He is very energetic. If you ever had a project like Habitat for Humanity or March of Dimes or you wanted to take a company to the stock exchange, he's the kind of guy you'd want leading the charge.

"And sometimes Henry reminds me more of Pop than his real sons. A big strong guy. Look at his hands, you can tell he's not afraid of work. Henry is quiet and doesn't say much. But when he talks, people listen. When I get agitated with Doug or Melvin about something they are doing, I will turn to Henry and say 'You gotta do something with these guys,'" Frascogna laughs.

"All of them have quite a wallop when it comes to influencing others and they derive their power from different sources, just as their personalities are different. And superimposed on everything they do is the same level of courtesy and equanimity that they learned from Mom and Pop Williams all these years. There is just a certain class surrounding everything they do.

"I've seen in little things, such as when we are in a business meeting together, where Henry, Doug, and Melvin are actually the centerpiece of that meeting. And sometimes in the flow of conversation someone will get excited and start interrupting and I have always noticed that they will always back off and let that other person talk. It's just a simple show of respect for the other person. It is also the characteristic of someone who has a deep, deep confidence in themselves."

By the late 1980s, The Williams Brothers had sold many a record for the labels they had signed with: ABC/Songbird, Nashboro, Savoy, Tomato, New Birth, Word, Malaco, and Light. When Leonard brought up the idea of starting their own label, both Melvin and Doug were enthusiastic. It would mean some extra responsibilities for promoting their own projects, but then again, the extra profits would mean more security for their families. The timing, however, wasn't right for Doug, Melvin, and Henry.

In 1988, after much discussion, Leonard decided to leave the group and start a company, Melendo Records, in Jackson. (Melvin, Leonard, and Doug had already started a music publishing company by the same name, taking parts of their first names to form the name Melendo.) The parting was amiable: No family member was ever made to feel that he couldn't try new projects when he saw opportunities. Leonard, his wife Billie Jean, and their two children, Leonard Jr. (nicknamed "LaMorris") and Amanda, had already moved to Jackson, Mississippi, at that time. Leonard went on to form another group in Jackson called The Chosen Generation, featuring Leonard himself, Theodore Cross, and LaMorris.

In 1991, after Leonard had been away from the group for three years, Melvin, Henry, and Doug decided the time was right to form their own record label. Their attorney, Mike Frascogna, who had actually written a book about musical artist management, advised them against it.

"You guys are very good at what you do; you are excellent songwriters and performers. But traditionally, artists don't do well at starting a record label. Go ahead and be a production company and produce your songs and albums and others' songs and albums. But don't get into something like a record company, a business that can devour you even if you're a good businessman."

The three met with similar responses from an executive friend at Malaco Records, the record label where they were recording at that time, only the negatives were even stronger. The exec didn't mince words: "If you [try to start a company] now, you'll be dead in the water." If he had known them just a little bettter, he might have realized that his words would make Doug, Melvin, and Henry more determined than ever to carry out their plans—and to succeed.

"He was probably basing his opinion on the fact that most artists are unsuccessful when starting a label," Doug remembers. "As musicians, they might gladly stay up all night working on a song in the studio but when it comes to business details like pro formas and contracts and budgets, most artists don't have what it takes to hang in there."

They knew that starting a record label wouldn't be easy. Doug, the planner of the family, awoke nights with anxiety attacks and pains deep in the pit of his stomach. Melvin lost weight worrying about what taking that step would mean to them. They knew that what they wanted to do was a wise move. It was a vision from God. When the day came for them to stop performing, they would still have the security of a business, one in which they could sell records for other groups that they signed. But still the *fact* of making such a decision was huge.

Finally, they called brother Frank (at the time, he had already become director of the Gospel Division for Malaco). Frank gave them the soundest advice he could think of.

"Trust the Lord, and trust yourselves. If you think you are ready, then you are ready. I'll help you any way I can."

The easiest step was to name the label.

Years before, when they started their booking agency, they had called it

Blackberry Entertainment. They decided to use "Blackberry" again, and called their new record company Blackberry Records. At the same time, they came up with the tag, "The Blacker the Berry, the Sweeter the Music." It was settled. "Let's show them that we may have grown up country boys, but when it comes to music, we know what we are doing," Doug said.

Another sign that convinced them they were making the right decision was the response they were getting from their most recent albums.

If there was anything The Williams Brothers could do, it was sell records. Fourteen of their seventeen albums had charted among the top ten in *Billboard* and *Cashbox* magazines. Three songs had gone to number one. Average sales of their albums were between 50,000 and 150,000 units per release, very respectable numbers in the world of gospel music.

Their expertise as songwriters, performers, and musicians was never questioned. It was the handling of the business side that worried McComb bankers. For weeks, the three leaders of the group went to every bank in town trying to secure the nearly $100,000 they needed to start the label.

"We've known you all your lives," they kept hearing, "and we'd really like to lend you the money, but we're not sure it's a sound investment. It's the music business. How can you guarantee profits on something so speculative as selling records?"

The Williams Brothers' twenty-year track record in the music industry didn't seem to mean anything to the bankers. Although they were discouraged, the trio never lost their faith in another of Pop's rules for life, the one that said you "can't have your own" without staying power. In the summer of 1991, a miracle happened. Returning to the office after yet another rejection, they made a phone call to a friend in Memphis, a businessman. The friend, a long-time fan of The Williams Brothers, believed wholeheartedly in the spiritual message the group conveyed each time they sang. "I want to help," he told Melvin. The very next day, Doug remembers, "He went to the bank and got a $50,000 loan. He told us, 'It's yours. You guys are going to make it.'"

But the Lord wasn't through blessing yet. They still needed more capital to get the company rolling.

A few days later Doug Williams called another friend, about something unrelated to their search for funds, and more good news came. "I heard what you guys want to do," the friend said. "I'll give you $20,000, but it has to be just between us." Doug was flabbergasted. He didn't know what to say, except to blurt thanks to his friend, then send a prayer skyward to thank God for the miracle that had just been sent to them.

They now had enough money to get started. Doug was named president and CEO of the label with Henry as vice-president and Melvin as secretary and treasurer. Marilyn joined in as administrative assistant (she was to become vice-president of operations six years, later, in 1997) and Thomas Saulsberry was brought on board as marketing/promotions director. Blackberry Records was ready to go.

Like any child, the new company had to go through a learning process. The Williams Brothers knew the music business—how to write and perform and even the technical aspects of producing a record. It was the other part, the business part, they would have to learn now.

All the details that had been handled by someone else—budgeting for a recording session, paying for studio time, photography and graphics for promotion, travel expenses—were now their responsibility. Fortunately, The Williams Brothers had two tremendous assets going for them. First, they were not afraid to work. They had spent too many hot afternoons picking cotton or mixing mortar to complain about long hours and difficult tasks. And second, they were fast learners. It didn't take long for them to add words and phrases like "profit and loss," "revenue," and "bottom line" to their vocabularies.

At the time, some people might have been surprised that Doug, the youngest of the ten children born to Leon and Amanda Williams, was the one to become president of the record company. But no one who truly knew Doug would have been surprised. His style wasn't loud and sometimes flamboyant like that of his father. He had, however, inherited Pop's ability to juggle several tasks at a time. And, as it turned out, he had the "staying power" to make sure everything fell into place, whether it was making sure all the text on an album's liner notes were grammatical or a performance contract for a concert in front of thousands of people had all the tees crossed and the i's dotted.

Nothing was too insignificant for the new business executive's attention.

"I'm thankful they didn't listen to my advice now," says Mike Frascogna. "Unlike many artists who, when trying to start a record label, want to jump and do it all, they have stayed within themselves. That means, they have known their own strengths and weaknesses and have tried to keep doing what they do best, then turn over aspects of running the company, like legal issues, to other people. I think they learned that from Pop. They have put a lot of faith in their sister Marilyn to be the front-line person in the office while they are out on the road."

That is not to say the effort of starting the new company didn't take its toll as The Williams Brothers learned the ropes. Doug, especially, felt the strain.

"There have been times when I felt like throwing up my hands, but we have just had this determination to make it work. I am the kind of person, that once I decide on something, I am going to see it through," says Doug. "But I had plenty of sleepless nights with all the tension and stress in my neck and shoulders, to the point of putting me in the hospital briefly. I was just trying to put too much on myself.

"At first, I was trying to do too much because I thought I had to, as president of the company. But then I started thinking about the songs we sang, songs that said things like 'Take it to the Lord in prayer and leave it there.'

I realized I needed to start letting some of these songs minister to me like they had ministered to other people. I prayed to the Lord then and told him 'Lord, this is in your hands. I've done all I can do.' Then the burden started lifting off my shoulders. I guess He was waiting until I decided to turn it back over to Him."

Doug remembers that one of the songs he sang as a duet with Yolanda Adams on his solo album *Heartsongs,* "After the Storm," was particularly meaningful:

After the storm has come and gone—after the wind
Has already blown
After the clouds have cleared the sky
God's going to wipe these tears from my eyes
After the storm

There have been days—when I've hurt so bad
The load on my shoulders—seemed much more than I
Could stand
There have been times—when the pain inside
Was so severe—I'd just sit alone and cry
Then a voice spoke to me—it was ever so gently
Saying you're gonna make it thru—that storm
That's hovering over you

These heartaches I feel—are just temporary
The storm is passing over—I see the sun breaking
Thru the clouds
There's a new day coming—and it won't be long
There will be a rainbow in the sky—and I'll have
A brand new song
I'll shout troubles over—and rejoice in victory

I'm gonna sail on peaceful waters — there's a
Brighter day for me

I've gotta keep my head up high — no matter how
Hard it seems
I've gotta keep on pressing on — Though the road's
Been rough for me
I will not, I shall not — I just can't give up the
Race
For God is on my side — Yes God is on my side

And it's gonna be alright — after the storm has
Come and gone *

Even though their attorney had advised them against starting the record company, he still represented The Williams Brothers in all their legal affairs, just as he had promised Pop Williams twenty years earlier. Doug, Melvin, and Henry wanted Frascogna to play a bigger role, however. They wanted him to also represent Blackberry Records and to oversee the overall business affairs for the new record company.

At first, he declined. He had been involved in the entertainment industry years earlier in a management and promotion capacity, having started in college booking bands for the fraternity houses. Even though he enjoyed his long-standing relationship with The Williams Brothers, Frascogna felt he didn't want to become so directly involved in the hands-on part of the entertainment industry again. But The Williams Brothers insisted that he think it over.

Doug called Mike one day and invited him to come with the group to New York for the 1992 Grammy Awards show. The group had been

* | *Written by Doug Williams. Courtesy Dalf Music Company.*

nominated for a Grammy for their 1991 album *This Is Your Night*. Mike agreed to accept their invitation to travel to New York for the awards show, on the stipulation that he bring his 14-year-old son Marty along.

Once in New York, Mike and Marty were caught up in the buzz of excitement that always surrounds the event. Even though The Williams Brothers were a gospel group and not among the most famous celebrities at the awards ceremony, Mike thought it would be fun for his son—and for him—to see some of the big-name music stars that would be on hand. And see them they did.

As they were standing outside their hotel in their tuxedos waiting for the limousine to take them to Radio City Music Hall, Mike noticed people stopping by to greet Doug and Henry and Melvin.

"Hey, do you know who that is?" Mike asked Marty, pointing at the woman who was chatting with The Williams Brothers. "That's Gladys Knight!"

Marty, staring blankly, said,"Who's that?" Mike just shook his head.

One after another, several longtime friends and famous performers and songwriters stopped by to say hello to the group. Marty knew none of them, which was not surprising considering that he was from a different generation, and had a different musical taste. But Mike was growing more and more amazed. He had known that The Williams Brothers were well known outside the state of Mississippi, but he was just beginning to fully realize the extent of their fame.

A few minutes passed as the Frascogna father and son hung on the fringes of the crowd around The Williams Brothers. Mike happened to look down at Marty at one point and noticed his mouth was hanging open. He was wordlessly pointing at a young man who was telling Doug how much he enjoyed their music.

"Dad, do you know who that is?" Marty said in hushed tones of reverence.

Mike shook his head. He had no idea who the young man with the baggy jeans, sunglasses, and baseball hat was.

"That's LL Cool J!" Marty said, still watching the famous rap performer (and soon-to-be television star) talking to The Williams Brothers.

Right then, The Williams Brothers had a new young fan.

After they arrived at the auditorium, as they stepped out of the limo the crowd gathered near the roped-off entrance immediately began applauding and shouting the names of Henry, Melvin, and Doug. They were led to their seats in the fifth row, right next to Bonnie Raitt (another Williams Brothers fan, they discovered). As they waited for the show to begin, a stream of well-known artists from all corners of the music universe stopped to greet the group.

"I'm thinking to myself, 'I guess I didn't really know how big these guys are in their genre.' I guess I was like most people in Mississippi who think, yes, these are The Williams Brothers, nice guys from Smithdale, Mississippi; just Doug, Melvin, and Henry. But go to Radio City Music Hall with them, and even though they are still the same humble guys, you realize how big they are," Mike remembers, smiling. "Looking back on that experience, I think that they knew what they were doing, in their quiet way. They knew I was ambivalent about being a part of the record company, so I think they wanted me to get a better idea of the big picture. And I did."

Soon after, Mike invited Doug, Melvin, and Henry to his home for an evening meeting that stretched into the wee hours as they talked about every angle and every dream that this young Blackberry Records company had. Soon, Frascogna was on board with the record label, advising them on their business strategies and overseeing many of the business and personnel decisions.

Before finishing *This Is Your Night*—and before Frascogna joined the company—Blackberry Records had secured a distributor—someone to get their records from the warehouse to the retailers who would actually sell them to fans. In the past, the record companies they had signed with had come to them with package deals that included distribution as well as production and promotion of their records. As their own record company, they felt that they should contract with an independent distributor to handle that part of the business.

Bob McKenzie, owner of Spectra Distribution in Nashville, made an attractive bid and invited the trio to his city to see Spectra's operation. Less than a week later, a distribution deal was signed.

Now they just needed something to distribute. There was never any question that the first album to bear the Blackberry label would be a Williams Brothers album.

Melvin and Doug worked for months writing songs to go on their debut album. The recording session in Chicago was especially hard on Melvin, who worked long hours in the studio, making sure that everything was right. In almost record time, eleven cuts were ready but the album needed one more song.

A tune had been playing in Melvin's head since they had arrived in Chicago. One evening after a particularly grueling session, he sat down with his guitar in the studio to relax. He wasn't thinking about the song; he just started playing, and his tune became a whole song. He called Doug over and played it for him. "That's great. Let's put it on the album," Doug said.

"I don't have any words for it," Melvin replied. "Let me work on it for a while and see what I can come up with."

Doug agreed and before they left the studio that night, Melvin had laid down the music tracks for the new song. Doug had seen his brother write great songs in such a short time before, and he knew he could do it again. What he didn't realize was that Melvin was troubled.

It was like the whole world had landed on him that night. When he got back to the hotel and sat alone in his room to finish the song, Melvin just couldn't force the words to come out. He thought about everything except the song. He relived his father's death and funeral; he struggled again to discover where he had gone wrong in his marriage that had just ended in divorce after a year's separation; he worried about his daughter LaTonya and her battle against sickle cell anemia.

Now he had to write this song and it had to be good for their new album. Everyone was depending on him and there was so much at stake. He worried that it wouldn't be good enough.

There was just one place for him to turn.

He went to his suitcase and took out his Bible. In the middle of the floor in his hotel room, Melvin got on his knees and ask the Lord to help him. And He did. The song that came to him was to be called "Prayer Made the Difference":

> *Many times in my life, I've come through the storm and rain,*
> *And time after time in my life, I've overcome heartaches and pain,*
> *But I've always kept faith in God 'cuz I knew somehow He would*
> *make a way.*
> *I kept trusting and kept believing and I always prayed.*
> *You see, through prayer, God strengthened me and made me strong.*
> *Prayer gave me the courage to keep on keeping on.*
>
> *Prayer made the difference,*
> *If it comes through by prayer, prayer changes things.*
>
> *Prayer's been a shoulder for me to lean on.*
> *Prayer's been a comforter when it seemed like hope was gone.*
> *It's been my rock, my salvation and prayer has been my shield.*
> *If it's God's will there is no wound that prayer can't heal.*

You see, through prayer, God strengthened me and made me strong.
Prayer gave me the courage to keep on keeping on.

Prayer made the difference,
If it comes through by prayer, prayer changes things. *

The next morning Melvin walked into the studio where Doug, Henry, and the musicians were waiting. He played the song for them, this time with the words that God had given him. They recorded it a few hours later.

The album *This Is Your Night* was released shortly thereafter and quickly rose to #4 on the *Billboard* charts, with the songs "Prayer Made the Difference" and "How I Depend on You" getting a good deal of play nationally on gospel radio. In 1991, Blackberry had its first hit with the first album on the new label. Not only was the album nominated for a Grammy, but it helped The Williams Brothers receive a Stellar Award for Best Performance Group or Duo (Traditional) in 1991.

The young record company was determined not to repeat the mistakes of other artists who had started their own record companies only to have themselves as the only client. From the start, they searched for other artists that would record on Blackberry. They weren't satisfied, however, to accept just any artist on their label. All their years in the industry told The Williams Brothers exactly the type of artist they were looking for. It would take more than just musical talent for someone to be added to the Blackberry roster. If you recorded for Blackberry, you had to display a special relationship with God, an anointing.

Hundreds of tapes began coming into the Blackberry offices following the success of *This Is Your Night*. Doug, Melvin, and Henry spent weeks listening to them all.

When it came time to choose another artist for the label, however, they

---

* | © *1991 Melvin Williams Music.*

didn't have to look far. Just a few miles north of Jackson on I-55 was the town of Canton, Mississippi. That was the home of Harvey Watkins, Sr., and his son Harvey, Jr., who were part of a group called the Canton Spirituals.

The Watkins had been longtime friends of the Williams family. In fact, the two groups had often performed together on the same bill. Harvey, Jr. had grown up knowing and admiring Doug and Melvin. The Canton Spirituals had been recording for J&B Records, but quickly accepted when Blackberry asked them to become part of their new family.

Another group they signed was Pastor Murphy Pace and The Voices of Power, from Atlanta. The Williams Brothers had performed with Pastor Pace's sisters, The Annointed Pace Sisters, many times over the years. Blackberry knew that The Voices of Power was the kind of group they wanted on their label.

One incident with Pace and The Voices of Power showed that Blackberry Records was open to different musical styles, if the message was in tune with their vision.

While working on his second album for the label, Pace gave Blackberry Records the opportunity to record a most unusual song. Pace spent much of his time ministering to the homeless in Atlanta. One day, while in an alley near the downtown area, he met Clyde Strozier. Strozier had come to America a year earlier from Jamaica and had been unable to find work or a home. What kept him going was a deep and abiding faith.

Pastor Murphy Pace liked the man and helped find someone who could take him in. As a way of thanking him, Clyde wrote a song for Pace:

> *I can feel the love of Jesus . . . All over me.*
> *I can feel the love of Jesus . . . All over me.*
> *I can feel it in my hands . . . It's all over me.* *

---

* | © *1994 Pop's Dream Music.*

It was unlike anything Pace had ever heard, a gospel song with a reggae beat. During a live recording session in Atlanta, Pace invited Strozier in, not only to be part of the recording but to sing the song himself for the Voices of Power album *Strong Holds,* backed by Pastor Pace's Voices of Power choir. They were struck by the sincerity and simplicity of Clyde's words.

With The Canton Spirituals and The Voices of Power as part of their lineup, The Williams Brothers were feeling like Blackberry Records would be a success. They were right. It didn't take long for the new label to build its catalog of albums. In 1992, Blackberry released Melvin's second solo album, *In Living Color,* which received a Stellar nomination, plus two collections of various artists, *Down Home Christmas in Mississippi* and *Gospel Showcase*. In 1993 came *The Best Of and More—Live,* a live performance of The Williams Brothers' past hits, plus *Christmastime at Blackberry* by various artists. In 1994, another Williams Brothers album, *In This Place,* sold very well on the strength of two songs: "In A Very Big Way" and "Cover Me." Also in 1994, Blackberry released *Songs Mama Used to Sing* by various artists, followed in 1995 by *Gospel Night in New Orleans* and Doug's first solo project, *Heartsongs,* which had the hit single "Living Testimony." In 1996, *Blackberry's Greatest Hits—Vol. 1* was released, and in 1997 came *Still Standing,* which featured the song "Waitin' on Jesus" and a guest appearance by Stevie Wonder in the old spiritual, "I'm Too Close." The most recent releases by Blackberry, in 1998, were Melvin's third solo album, *Never Seen Your Face,* and *A Candlelight Christmas* by The Williams Brothers.

But at the beginning of 1993, when thousands of copies of *The Best of and More—Live* were still sitting in the warehouse, once again their lives would be changed with a phone call.

CHAPTER X 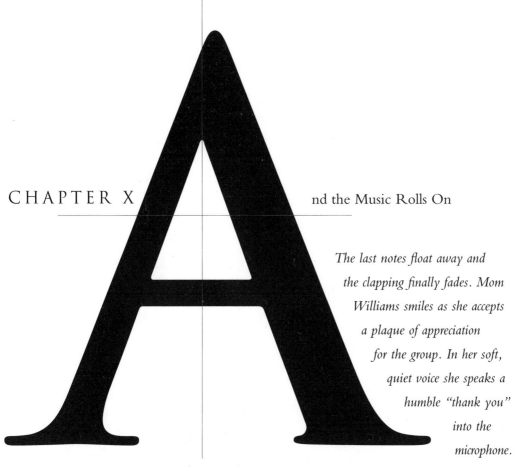 nd the Music Rolls On

The last notes float away and the clapping finally fades. Mom Williams smiles as she accepts a plaque of appreciation for the group. In her soft, quiet voice she speaks a humble "thank you" into the microphone.

The family mingles in the parking lot after the service, saying hello to old friends. Amanda and Marilyn don't linger too long, however. It's time to hurry home to get The Big House ready. After all, what is a homecoming without a family dinner.

One by one they arrive.

Mom is content to rest her arthritic legs as she sits on the sofa in the living room. She squeezes hands and accepts the hugs as friends and family fill her house with laughter and conversation.

They are filling their plates from the kitchen table with Marilyn's macaroni and cheese, Ree's fried chicken, and Deliana's vegetable casserole.

People are everywhere, plopped on the couch, eating around the dining room table or sitting on the floor with their plates. Peals of laughter erupt from this small group or that as they relive memories.

This is the way Mom loves to see her family.

She is visiting with the preacher who has come by to pay his respects, when voices from the den catch her attention.

"Did you feel the Lord there with us tonight?" someone asks.

Amanda hears Josie Marie's firm reply: "I sure did, and you know, I think Pop was there with Him."

It was early in January 1993. Melvin, Doug, and Henry were sitting in Mike Frascogna's office. They'd just gotten home from their latest weekend concert when Mike Frascogna called and asked them to come to his office in Jackson for a meeting. The trio was quietly waiting for Mike to find the right words to tell them his news. They could tell from his face that it was not good news.

"I'm just going to come straight out," he said. "I don't know how else to do it than to just say it." He took a deep breath. "I got a call from your distributor's attorneys yesterday. Spectra has gone bankrupt. They are completely broke. Apparently they didn't tell anyone anything until it had already happened." At that time, Spectra owed Blackberry nearly $90,000 from records they had already sold. The money was lost to them, but much more was at stake. Tens of thousands of Blackberry records were sitting at the Spectra warehouse, and record stores across the United States were waiting for them. A bankruptcy proceeding could tie up those albums, and put Blackberry Records out of business.

Doug felt like someone had punched him in the stomach. Those pains he'd had just before they started the label were back. Melvin found his voice first. "What about everything that is waiting to be released?"

"It's in their warehouse," Mike said. "There's just no way for them to fill the orders coming in from the record stores."

"But there are 40,000 to 50,000 pieces of the new album just sitting there," Henry said.

"Hopefully, it won't take long to find a new distributor," Frascogna said. He had already arranged for trucks to be dispatched to the Spectra warehouses where the Blackberry albums were stored. The product was loaded on to the trucks and moved to other storage sites under Blackberry's control. Frascogna's quick action was to pay off in the near future.

The sudden blow of Spectra's folding, however, was numbing to Melvin, Henry, and Doug. This could deal a death blow to the young record company. No one said a word as they drove back to McComb. No one knew what to say.

Doug called Bob McKenzie at Spectra the minute they got back. Two days later Bob returned his call. "What happened?" Doug asked.

"I'm just real sorry," McKenzie said. Not then, or any day later, did McKenzie ever offer any kind of explanation.

The rest of the week was a blur. Still in shock, the people at Blackberry Records carried on their usual activities, operating purely by instinct. The group packed up the bus and left for their weekend performances as they always had. When they came back, they were ready for action.

The following Monday, the phones began ringing in the offices early. Everyone was fielding calls from other distributors who had heard the news and wanted the chance to make a deal with Blackberry. Melvin and Doug contacted a few other companies they thought would match their way of doing business, and in the middle of the week, they got on a plane and flew to Nashville to meet with Word Records.

The Word offer wasn't exactly what they wanted but they had to seriously consider it. Record stores were clamoring for Blackberry products and the longer they were out of commission, the worse the problem would become. Not only had Spectra's bankruptcy hurt Blackberry financially; their professional credibility was at stake.

Something was happening to Frank Williams as he sang a solo of the traditional hymn "Amazing Grace" during the recording of The Mississippi Mass Choir's latest album *It Remains to Be Seen*.

Suddenly he wasn't the man whose two-year battle with the debilitating lung disease blastomycosis had destroyed 90 percent of his lungs. He wasn't even in the recording studio any more, surrounded by the 120 members of the choir he had created. Instead his stool was perched on a cloud, and he was singing the song for an audience of one, the Lord Himself. The two of them were having a personal conversation.

No one in the choir dared move or say a word for fear of interrupting. They had seen this happen before. They had all witnessed Frank getting ready to go on stage for a performance. They had seen his small thin frame double over as he was wracked by his frequent coughing spells. But when he stepped on stage to sing there was no sign of the illness that had forced him to cut back on his performance schedule. The nagging cough disappeared. When Frank Williams sang it was as though he was getting his breath and energy from God himself. (The other song he recorded that night, "Your Grace and Mercy," received the Song of the Year Award at the 1993 Gospel Music of America's Excellence Awards and went on to become one of the most popular gospel songs ever.)

Shortly after the recording session, Frank walked into the small office he shared with choir business manager Jerry Mannery at Malaco Records.

"I want to go with the choir to Savannah on March 20," he said. "Make the arrangements please."

Jerry didn't hesitate a second before picking up the phone to call the promoter in Georgia. It had been months since Frank had felt like going out with the choir. If Frank wanted to go to Savannah, Jerry wouldn't do anything to stand in his way.

The promoter was more than happy to send a plane ticket for Frank. But Frank also made sure to be there at the bus as usual when the rest of the choir was ready to pull out of Jackson for the trip. As always, he led the group in prayer, asking the Lord to bless the bus and the choir and grant them a safe journey. He smiled at Katrina and his two children who were traveling on the bus. They were excited because they didn't usually get to travel with the choir on trips like this. Frank hugged them and waved at the bus as it rolled away.

He flew out the next day, almost beating the choir there, and spent a quiet Saturday afternoon exploring Savannah with his family. The next day, he ignored the usual buzz of activity that preceded every choir concert, choosing to spend the time before the performance in prayer and meditation in his dressing room. His friend Reverend Cone stuck his head in the door and then spent the next few minutes with Frank on his knees. By the time he took the stage, Frank was ready to sing.

And sing he did. This time, not only the choir but the entire Civic Auditorium crowd saw the unique and inspirational relationship Frank had with the Lord as he sang "Near the Cross" like a man with two healthy lungs. Frank finished the song and the entire auditorium erupted into applause and shouts of "Amen!" Frank walked over and took a seat next to pianist Jerry Smith. He smiled and said to Jerry, "I'm back."

Everyone felt it was a special evening, even for a Mass Choir program. After the concert, Frank went out to eat dinner with his family and spoke to nearly everyone on his way in to join Katrina and the children at their table. As they waited for their dinner, Katrina could tell Frank was distracted. He kept turning his head in the direction of Reverend Cone and the group of men he was with. They were deep in discussion about the Bible, and Frank was straining to hear them.

Finally, Katrina gave him a look as if to say, "Go on." Frank smiled and said "I won't be long," but she knew better. If there was anything Frank loved better than singing gospel, it was talking about the Lord. He would talk for hours to anyone and everyone who would listen. And this time was no exception.

In fact, after he put his family on the bus that evening and prayed again for the choir on their return trip, he spent the entire night in prayer and reading scriptures. When Jerry Mannery called the hotel the next morning, Frank was on the phone telling Reverend Cone about his night of fellowship with the Lord.

"I feel at peace," he told the reverend. "I feel better than I have for months." Then he left for the airport for the return flight to Jackson.

At the same time, Katrina and the children were getting off the bus in Jackson. As they drove out of the parking lot in their car, she let the children choose where they wanted to eat breakfast. Of course, they chose McDonald's. Before they could get out of the restaurant parking lot, young Frankie began shivering uncontrollably. Katrina pulled the car over and pulled him onto her lap as she continued her drive home. The shaking diminished some as she did her best to drive the car with one hand while holding her son tightly. When they got home, she put him to bed. Suddenly the shaking stopped; he was fine.

At virtually the same time back in Georgia, a crowd was gathering around Frank. Paramedics were trying to revive him there at the airport gate where he had collapsed shaking and shivering, unable to breathe. He was loaded onto a stretcher and rushed to a hospital.

Jerry Mannery, who had waited for Frank's flight in Jackson, went back to his office when Frank didn't get off the plane, assuming he had missed the plane. He had just sat down at his desk when the phone rang.

"Frank collapsed at the airport," said Bryan Williams, Linder's husband.

Jerry immediately called the hospital, and after many delays, was able to get the doctor on the line.

"Mr. Williams is in very serious condition. We are trying to get him stabilized," the doctor said.

At that moment, another line lit up. It was Katrina. Jerry told her to meet him at his office. He was waiting there for her with Malaco president Tommy Couch. Katrina had just walked in the door when the doctor called back.

The look on Jerry's face told it all. The doctors had been unable to revive Frank. The official cause of death was acute cardiorespiratory arrest.

Frank was brought home to Jackson for the funeral. At dawn on March 27, 1993, a crowd began gathering at the Greater Bethlehem Temple Church. It was to be the kind of send-off he would have loved.

By the time the service began, nearly 5,000 people had arrived, filling and overflowing the large church. There wasn't a dry eye among the members of The Mississippi Mass Choir as they sang for Frank, joined by artists Dorothy Norwood, Reverend James Moore, Bishop Walter Hawkins, R&B singer Johnny Taylor, Reverend Art Jones of The Florida Mass Choir, and Reverend Milton Biggham, executive director of Savoy Records in New York. Reverend Cone and others took turns praising Frank as a pioneer and innovator in gospel music.

The story of Frank Williams life and death appeared on the front page of *The Clarion-Ledger,* a newspaper with statewide distribution. Kenneth Dupre, editor-in-chief of *Score* magazine, was to write, "Frank Williams was one of the greatest champions of gospel music."

The choir began a rousing rendition of "Joy Is Going to Come in the Morning" and everyone joined in. Reverend Biggham began clapping in time to the song and soon every person there was clapping. Inside and outside the church, the friends and family of Frank Williams clapped loudly and sang loudly. Neighbors in the houses near the church came out into their yards to listen to this heavenly sound.

All around, tears gave way to smiles. They were smiling at the thought of

Frank finally having his conversation with the Lord, face to face.

In the middle of the crisis at Blackberry Records caused by their lack of a distributor, Doug, Melvin, and Henry took time out to attend the funeral of their former brother-in-law Willie Banks (Willie and Deliana had been divorced in 1973). As they got out of their cars and walked toward the church to pay their respects, they ran into Tommy Couch, who was coming out of the church. Tommy shared his condolences with the brothers, reminiscing about the great times he had shared with Willie, Frank, and his brothers. As he was getting into his car, Tommy asked, "Have you found a distributor yet?"

Doug shook his head. "No, we haven't found what we want yet."

Tommy stopped. "Why haven't you talked to us?"

Doug was surprised. He assumed that since Malaco wasn't handling production of The Williams Brothers' records, the company would not be interested in a distribution deal. (Up to that time Malaco had distributed only its own artists.) But Malaco was ready to make an exception, and a deal was struck not long after Doug's encounter with Tommy. It wasn't long before the Blackberry warehouse inventory was on its way to record stores again.

"I think that Malaco agreed to distribute another record company's product for two reasons," explains Mike Frascogna. "First, we had the product on hand immediately, because we had rescued all those albums from the warehouses at Spectra before the bankruptcy. And second, I think that Tommy Couch respected the work of Frank Williams, who had basically given Malaco a foundation in the gospel music market in years past."

More awards and recognition were to come to The Williams Brothers and Blackberry Records. In January 1995, their release entitled *In This Place* reached number one on the *Billboard* charts, was nominated for a Grammy Award in the category of Best Soul Gospel Album, and won a Stellar Award for Best Performance by Group or Duo (Traditional). Doug also received a

Grammy nomination and two Stellars—Male Vocalist of the Year and Contemporary Male Vocalist of the Year—for his solo project, *Heartsongs,* which was also recorded in 1995.

In 1997, a series of events was to give The Williams Brothers an even wider range of exposure than they had ever known before.

Some friends of the group also happened to be friends of pop superstar Stevie Wonder. When these mutual friends heard Wonder talking about possibly recording some gospel, they spoke up. Wonder needed to get The Williams Brothers involved in the project, they told him.

In early 1997, when Wonder was performing in New Orleans, a casual meeting was arranged at the hotel where the star was staying. Doug was out of town at the time, but Melvin and Henry went up to Stevie's suite and sat around the baby grand piano in the room, talking and singing a bit. The old spiritual "I'm Too Close" had been one of Wonder's favorites since childhood. When they started humming and singing that song, Melvin mentioned to him that he would love to include a performance by Wonder of "I'm Too Close" on the next Williams Brothers project. Stevie laughed and said he was saving that song for himself to record one day. They began singing other songs, but eventually came back to his favorite again. Before the meeting/song session was over, Stevie had said he would "think about" doing the song with The Williams Brothers.

Through their mutual friends, Melvin kept in touch with Wonder's people. Eventually, he agreed to do the song. Both sides so enjoyed the experience of recording "I'm Too Close" (which was to become the second track on The Williams Brothers' most recent CD, *Still Standing*) that a video project was planned. The video of "I'm Too Close" was scheduled to run on the music television channels MTV, VH1, and BET. However, when Stevie Wonder was invited by VH1 for a special, *VH1 Honors "Save the Music,"* he insisted that they include The Williams Brothers in the show. That special, on which the group sang backup with Steve Winwood and James Taylor, introduced The Williams Brothers to an international audience. Prior to that appearance, they were frequently seen on *Bobby Jones Gospel* and *Video Gospel* on BET Television.

As a result of that exposure, The Williams Brothers were invited to join the Gospel Power 98 Tour, a 61-city gospel tour with an urban/contemporary feel that ran from January 1998 through the spring of 1998 and was one of the largest tours of its kind ever. On the tour, billed by promoters as a "Gospelmania," The Williams Brothers sang with other famous gospel acts such as Fred Hammond and Radical for Christ, Hezekiah Walker, Dottie Peoples, Jonathan Slocumb, Men of Standard, Marvin Sapp, and Vickie Winans, among others, at venues seating from 2,500 to 12,000.

As for Blackberry Records, a new office building in McComb was finished in the summer of 1998, affording everyone a little relief from the cramped rented offices they had endured for eight years. It also allowed the company to expand the marketing and promotions departments, and gave the label more wall space. They would need it for the seven Stellar Award nominations they received in 1998. Eventually, Blackberry plans to go after more popular gospel artists—artists with proven track records in sales—to include on the label.

Melvin's third solo album, *Never Seen Your Face,* was released in the spring of 1998. His second solo project for Blackberry Records, it included arrangements with backup by The Mississippi Mass Choir and collaborations with Marvin Winans of The Winans Family, Evangelist Shirley Caesar, Harvey Watkins Jr. of The Canton Spirituals, Bishop Tommie Lockett, and Paul Porter of the Christianaires.

Throughout The Williams Brothers' progression from a small local gospel group to one of the most well-known names in gospel music worldwide, one thing has remained constant: the true humility and compassion of the group's members and their basic decency as human beings.

Dennis Tobias, who has been associated with The Williams Brothers for almost 30 years, says, "I saw them grow from traveling in a car, then a van, then a bigger van, then a van pulling a trailer full of equipment, then a bigger trailer, then a small touring bus, then another bus even bigger. And as they have grown in stature as performers, they have always acknowledged their home, their family and their community. They are a group of guys who never let stardom go to their heads.

"A lot of professionals, when they start winning awards, don't have time for you anymore," says cousin Edward Cain. "They cut one demo in some backyard studio and you can't tell them which way is up after that. But not The Williams Brothers. They come by and speak to me and shake my hand, no matter if I'm dirty from working or what. They know how to maintain their professional status and how to treat their fellow man right. They haven't forgotten their roots."

Today, The Williams Brothers are involved in giving back to the McComb area communities through their involvement in several groups. Mission Pike County, a group of ministers who promote unity among black and white Christians and churches, have welcomed the group several times as performers for fund-raising functions. The annual Iron Horse Arts Festival in McComb has featured The Williams Brothers along with such artists as Ray Charles. The group has been involved in the Boys and Girls Clubs of the area, and the Blackberry Records offices proudly display trophies from the Little League sports teams they have sponsored

The Williams Brothers have also gone out of their way to encourage new young gospel groups as they are discovering their talents and their ministry. When Tobias was first managing his group, The Christianaires, one of the group's members asked, "Hey, can you ask Melvin Williams if he might come and give us some pointers?" The other group members said, "Nah, he won't have time for that kind of thing. He's too busy." A few nights later, the group was practicing at one of their homes and they heard a knock at the door. It was Melvin, with an armload of fried chicken and fixings. "I knew y'all probably didn't have time to slow for food, so I brought some. Now, let's get to work!"

What's ahead for The Williams Brothers?

Individually, they will certainly continue to lead full and satisfying lives.

Doug, Lavannah, and Ayannah, now in high school, live about two minutes from the new Blackberry office in McComb. Lavannah still teaches third grade at Eva Gordon Elementary, and is the one who takes Ayannah to piano lessons or to band practice where she plays clarinet. A basketball goal stands on one end of the circular driveway in front of their house, a hint of a one-time hobby of Doug's that he admits occupies little of his time these days. (At six feet two inches, Doug is the second tallest of the Williams children; only Huey, the third oldest child, is taller, at six feet three inches.)

The foyer of their home opens up to a family room with a twenty-foot ceiling and two large semicircular windows at the top through which pours whatever Mississippi sunshine is available at the moment. It's a comfortable home with an open layout, and when the Williams family comes for a visit, there seems to be a place for everyone. On the walls are a few mementos of the musical career but mostly this seems to be a place of refuge for the Williams extended family, any of whom are likely to pop by at any moment. (See the Williams Family Tree, on page 142.) The atmosphere is relaxed, a tone that owes much to the personal qualities of Blackberry's CEO.

Yet both admit that it has taken a tremendous effort to hold a family together with Doug being on the road so much. Especially in the early days the financial insecurities of the music business strained their relationship severely, and at times the pressure seemed almost overwhelming. Their commitment has held, however, through God's grace to them.

Melvin Williams lives in Smithdale, in one of the eight houses that now stand on the 100-acre plot Pop Williams bought back in the 1930s: his, his mother Amanda's (The Big House), Bill's (Leon Jr.'s), Deliana's, Huey's, Josie Marie's, niece Amanda's, and cousin Betty Ramsey's. "What better place to live," Melvin says, "than next to family?" His marriage to Donnice broke up in 1991, after ten years, but he regularly sees and talks to their teenage daughter LaTonya, who lives with her mother in McComb. (LaTonya is currently winning a battle against sickle-cell anemia.) Still a consummate music producer, he recently drove the 90 minutes from Smithdale to Malaco Records recording studio in Jackson (as he often has in the past) to work with his older brother Huey on the production of The Jackson Southernaires' latest project, *Warrior*.

Office work, or anything nonmusical that focuses on the same thing for hours, is not for Melvin. He prefers long hours in the recording studio or being on stage in a live performance. When he is making a new acquaintance or dealing with the sideline issues of the music business, Melvin's manner is as low-key and unself-conscious as his brother Doug's. It is when he is making music—as producer or performer—that his intensity reveals itself.

Studio musicians have been known to balk at what they sometimes consider Melvin's excessive demand for perfection in a song. And when working with his older brother, although he is patient and gentle, Melvin is still very much a perfectionist, often getting Huey to do take after take on a particularly challenging vocal phrase. Melvin's goal is to get the best out of the song, knowing that his brother—and the person who buys the CD and listens to it—expect all the details to meet and surpass their highest hopes.

During a performance, Melvin is everywhere, shouting to the crowd, doing whatever he can to stir them. He is all over the stage, dancing here, stopping and swaying a few seconds later, then punctuating the harmony of the rest of the group with his solo renderings. He is completely focused on getting the message of the music out to the people in that audience.

Melvin realizes that his single-mindedness was one of the main causes of the breakup of his marriage. Too much time on the road mixed with too little attention while at home were the destructive forces he set in motion. Some of the pain of his divorce has shown up in the songs he has recorded since then. Melvin is determined that if any good can come out of the mistakes he has made, it will be through his music.

Henry Green's life, like Melvin's, has had its high and low points. His first marriage at age 20, two years after joining The Little Williams Brothers, was to a Liberty, Mississippi girl, Willie Mae Thompson. Their relationship was stormy, and included angry scenes where she would wave a butcher knife at him to block him from leaving with Pop Williams on one of the singing trips that so often took him away from her. Henry and Willie Mae were divorced in 1971. His second marriage, to Freddye Thompson, lasted for over two decades, but also ended in divorce. Henry has two sons, Henry, Jr. and Brian, and stepson Timothy, all of whom he talks to regularly. He makes no excuses for what has happened, and, like many people who grew up poor, he doesn't dwell much on hardship.

Henry lives in McComb, in a suburban neighborhood, and in many ways there is a continuity between his life today and his childhood. Always, of course, there is music. But there are other echoes as well. He still loves vehicles (when he was a child, says his mother Ruth, "his main goal in life was to have his own car"), and he takes loving care of both a Mazda Millenia and a four-wheel drive Toyota truck. And in Henry's backyard is a sturdy enclosure where he keeps the Beagle dogs he has hand-trained for his beloved rabbit hunting, a passion he has pursued since he first learned to use a gun.

"Once you have a few dogs who know what they are doing," says Henry, "it's easy to train another one. You just put him out in the field and see if he knows how to work with the others and not stray off and do his own thing."

As Henry Green's personal and professional history attests, he is most definitely a man who "knows how to work with the others." Vice-president of Blackberry Records, Henry made the sacrifices and endured the hardships of the early days, sticking with The Williams Brothers even when he had doubts, and now, as always, when he speaks people listen.

As a group, The Williams Brothers plan to keep on making their own unique brand of gospel music and performing it for their fans.

Indeed, all three of The Williams Brothers agree that the most gratifying aspect of their work has been the reaction of their fans to the group's music. Melvin, Henry, and Doug have actually acted out the message of their music in loving people, embracing them for the Lord.

"We don't try to preach to people," says Doug. "We decided long ago just to deliver the message and put it out there and let people make the decision how they were going to accept it. We don't say 'You aren't good enough for this Gospel. We just put the message out there. And, in a lot of cases, people will come up and say 'That song you sang; it changed my life.' I have letters from guys in prison about how the Lord has used our songs to turn their lives around."

Doug remembers some touching feedback from fans also, recalling one incident in particular. "A man had a relative who had been unconscious, in a coma, and the family brought in one of our songs which was his favorite song called 'This May Be My Last Time' and played it over and over in the room, not even knowing if the man could hear it. Eventually he came out of the coma and when he did, he said that that song had helped pull him through it all.

"Being out on the road can be discouraging sometimes and get you down physically, mentally, emotionally, and even spiritually. But when someone comes up and tells you what an effect you have had in their life, it makes it all worthwhile. We know that what we are doing is not in vain."

One question often asked by people who love The Williams Brothers music is, Will their music ever cross over to a bigger audience? Some have called their style reminiscent of certain Motown performers from years past.

"Oftentimes I can close my eyes and listen to a Williams Brothers composition and it takes me back to those Motown sounds of my college years," says Frascogna. "Because of that, I think they have crossover appeal. If they ever happened to have a song or album that was the nexus of two markets, it would probably happen. Would they go out and do material to force a crossover? NO. They would never try to manipulate it. If it happens it will be because they are doing what they have always done: Sing their music the way it is given to them."

Frascogna points to a particular event, however, that let him know The Williams Brothers sound had great appeal to a more general audience. In 1995, the group was asked to perform the national anthem at the first National Football League game held in Jackson, Mississippi, in 25 years. A crowd of 55,000 people had gathered to watch a preseason game featuring the New York Jets against the Philadelphia Eagles. Mike had heard the group practice their rendition of the song, and it had brought chills as he listened. But he wasn't prepared for the reaction at the ballgame.

"At the end, when Henry hit that high note, 55,000 people erupted in applause and cheers," Frascogna says. "Not only that, but players from both teams—who had heard the national anthem probably hundreds of times before—came running up to The Williams Brothers to congratulate them and tell them how inspiring it was to them.

"Now, most of those people were probably not gospel fans, but The

Williams Brothers brought the house down. They are a powerful talent and a powerful presence."

As for Blackberry Records, the young company's catalog of releases continues to grow, which means the loyal fans of The Williams Brothers and the other artists on the label will look to Blackberry for years to come.

The first annual corporate meeting of Blackberry Records was held in the small village of Seaside on the Florida panhandle between Destin and Panama City in December 1997. In typical Williams Brothers fashion, their sweet dispositions and fun-loving natures won the town folks over in record time.

"We'd been having regular business meetings for several days, talking about the future of Blackberry and business strategies and so forth," Frascogna says. "Doug, Melvin, and Henry had spent plenty of time visiting here and there, especially at this little store called Modica Market, a central gathering place. Next thing I knew, I was at the store having breakfast when I heard a familiar Williams Brothers tune coming over the loudspeakers. And when the brothers got home, they sent back pictures to the Modica family. They just have that kind of effect on people."

The future for The Williams Brothers and for Blackberry Records is still bright. . .and still ahead.

And there is always the chance that the next generation of Williams children will let their musical talents shine for the Lord.

Amanda Cain Williams sits in her favorite chair at The Big House, hearing the chatter of all the family and friends spread everywhere as they enjoy the post-concert refreshments. She looks at her sons Doug and Melvin, then up at the photograph of her husband hanging on the wall across from her. She smiles and lets her eyes travel across the decorative brick arch her husband built in the living room years ago.

Yes, she tells herself, I believe Leon truly was here, patting both feet in time to the music.

DISCOGRAPHY

YEAR	TITLE	LABEL
1971	*He's My Brother* along with the Jackson Southernaires	Songbird
1973	*Holding On*	ABC/Songbird
1974	*What's Wrong With the People Today*	ABC/Songbird
1976	*Spreading a Message*	Nashboro
1977	*Taking Gospel Higher*	Savoy
1977	*Mama Prayed for Me*	Savoy
1978	*I've Got a Home*	Savoy
1978	*Celebrate This Christmas*	Savoy
1979	*First Class Gospel*	Tomato
1980	*God Will See You Through*	New Birth
1982	*Brother to Brother*	Word
1983	*Feel the Spirit*	Word
1985	*Blessed*	Malaco
1986	*Hand in Hand*	Malaco
1988	*A New Beginning*	Melendo
1988	*Back to the Cross* (Melvin Williams)	Light
1989	*Ain't Love Wonderful*	Malaco
1991	*This Is Your Night*	Blackberry
1991	*Tribute to Rev. James Cleveland, Vol. I* (Various Artists)	CGI
1992	*In Living Color, Live* (Melvin Williams)	Blackberry
1992	*Down Home Christmas in Mississippi* (Various Artists)	Blackberry
1992	*Gospel Showcase* (Various Artists)	Blackberry
1993	*The Best of and More, Live*	Blackberry
1993	*Christmastime at Blackberry* (Various Artists)	Blackberry
1994	*Songs Mama Used to Sing* (Various Artists)	Blackberry
1994	*In This Place*	Blackberry
1995	*Gospel Night in New Orleans* (Various Artists)	Blackberry
1995	*Heartsongs* (Doug Williams)	Blackberry
1996	*Together As One:* A Tribute to the Heritage of Quartet Music (Various Artists)	Intersound
1996	*Blackberry's Greatest Hits, Vol. I* (Various Artists)	Blackberry
1997	*Still Standing*	Blackberry
1998	*Never Seen Your Face* (Melvin Williams)	Blackberry
1998	*A Candlelight Christmas*	Blackberry

THE WILLIAMS

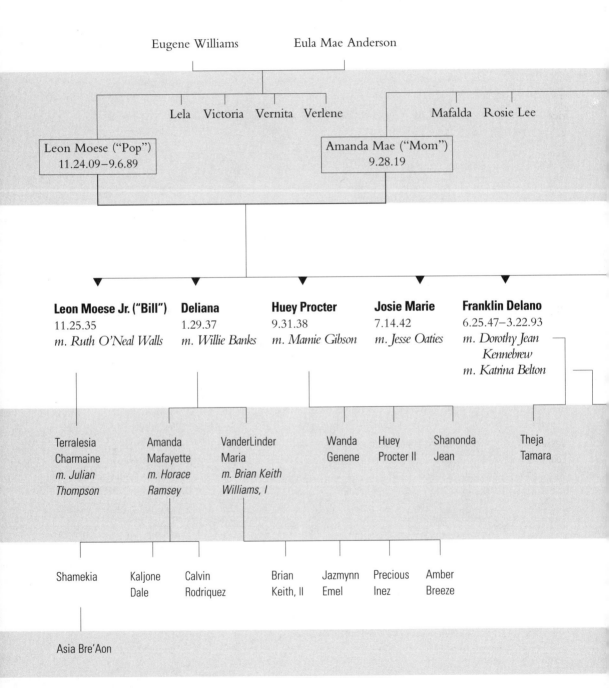

Eugene Williams   Eula Mae Anderson

Lela   Victoria   Vernita   Verlene   Mafalda   Rosie Lee

Leon Moese ("Pop")
11.24.09–9.6.89

Amanda Mae ("Mom")
9.28.19

Leon Moese Jr. ("Bill")
11.25.35
m. Ruth O'Neal Walls

Deliana
1.29.37
m. Willie Banks

Huey Procter
9.31.38
m. Mamie Gibson

Josie Marie
7.14.42
m. Jesse Oaties

Franklin Delano
6.25.47–3.22.93
*m. Dorothy Jean
Kennebrew*
m. Katrina Belton

Terralesia
Charmaine
*m. Julian
Thompson*

Amanda
Mafayette
*m. Horace
Ramsey*

VanderLinder
Maria
*m. Brian Keith
Williams, I*

Wanda
Genene

Huey
Procter II

Shanonda
Jean

Theja
Tamara

Shamekia

Kaljone
Dale

Calvin
Rodriquez

Brian
Keith, II

Jazmynn
Emel

Precious
Inez

Amber
Breeze

Asia Bre'Aon

FAMILY TREE

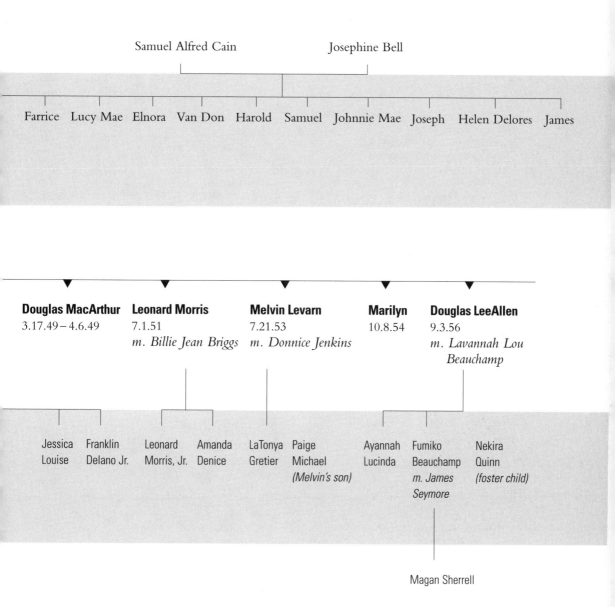

Samuel Alfred Cain   Josephine Bell

Farrice   Lucy Mae   Elnora   Van Don   Harold   Samuel   Johnnie Mae   Joseph   Helen Delores   James

Douglas MacArthur
3.17.49 – 4.6.49

Leonard Morris
7.1.51
m. Billie Jean Briggs

Melvin Levarn
7.21.53
m. Donnice Jenkins

Marilyn
10.8.54

Douglas LeeAllen
9.3.56
m. Lavannah Lou Beauchamp

Jessica Louise   Franklin Delano Jr.

Leonard Morris, Jr.   Amanda Denice

LaTonya Gretier   Paige Michael *(Melvin's son)*

Ayannah Lucinda   Fumiko Beauchamp *m. James Seymore*   Nekira Quinn *(foster child)*

Magan Sherrell

INDEX